Acting Antics

of related interest

Drama Therapy and Storymaking in Special Education
Paula Crimmens
ISBN-13: 978 1 84310 291 5   ISBN-10: 1 84310 291 9

**Dramatherapy for People with Learning Disabilities
A World of Difference**
Anna Chesner
Foreword by Sue Jennings
ISBN-13: 978 1 85302 208 1   ISBN-10: 1 85302 208 X

The Complete Guide to Asperger's Syndrome
Tony Attwood
ISBN-13: 978 1 84310 495 7   ISBN-10: 1 84310 495 4

**Asperger Syndrome
A Different Mind**
Simon Baron-Cohen
DVD
ISBN-13: 978 1 84310 471 1   ISBN-10: 1 84310 471 7

Social Skills Training for Adolescents with General Moderate Learning Difficulties
Ursula Cornish and Fiona Ross
ISBN-13: 978 1 84310 179 6   ISBN-10: 1 84310 179 3

Social Awareness Skills for Children
Márianna Csóti
ISBN-13: 978 1 84310 003 4   ISBN-10: 1 84310 003 7

People Skills for Young Adults
Márianna Csóti
ISBN-13: 978 1 85302 716 1   ISBN-10: 1 85302 716 2

**ISPEEK at Home
Over 1300 Visual Communication Images**
Janet Dixon
CD-Rom
ISBN-13: 978 1 84310 510 7   ISBN-10: 1 84310 510 1

**ISPEEK at School
Over 1300 Visual Communication Images**
Janet Dixon
CD-Rom
ISBN-13: 978 1 84310 511 4   ISBN-10: 1 84310 511 X

Self-Esteem Games for Children
Deborah Plummer
Illustrated by Jane Serrurier
ISBN-13: 978 1 84310 424 7   ISBN-10: 1 84310 424 5

Acting Antics

A Theatrical Approach to Teaching Social
Understanding to Kids and Teens
with Asperger Syndrome

Cindy B. Schneider

Jessica Kingsley Publishers
London and Philadelphia

First published in 2007
by Jessica Kingsley Publishers
116 Pentonville Road
London N1 9JB, UK
and
400 Market Street, Suite 400
Philadelphia, PA 19106, USA

www.jkp.com

Library of Congress Cataloging in Publication Data

Schneider, Cindy B., 1952-
Acting antics : a theatrical approach to teaching social understanding to kids and teens with Asperger syndrome / Cindy B. Schneider ; foreword by Tony Attwood ; illustrations by Shaan Pickett.
   p. ; cm.
Includes bibliographical references and index.
ISBN-13: 978-1-84310-845-0 (alk. paper)
ISBN-10: 1-84310-845-3 (alk. paper)
1. Asperger's syndrome—Patients—Education. 2. Asperger's syndrome—Social aspects. 3. Drama—Therapeutic use. 4. Social skills in children. 5. Social skills in adolescence. I. Title.
[DNLM: 1. Asperger Syndrome—therapy. 2. Adolescent. 3. Child. 4. Drama. 5. Psychodrama—methods. 6. Social Adjustment. WS 350.6 S358a 2007]
RJ506.A9S388 2007
618.92'858832—dc22

2006036354

British Library Cataloguing in Publication Data
A CIP catalogue record for this book is available from the British Library

ISBN-13: 978 1 84310 845 0
ISBN-10: 1 84310 845 3

Printed and bound in Great Britain by
Printwise (Haverhill) Ltd, Suffolk

*I would like to dedicate this book to the memory
of Marilyn Gerold, who inspired me as a young child
with the beauty and power of theater*

Acknowledgments

I would like to acknowledge many people who have encouraged and supported me throughout the writing of this book. My hubby and best friend, Ray, is my "roadie," my stage crew, and my constant support. My dear sister Susie has been my sounding board, my proof reader, and my cheerleader all through the writing process. I also want to thank my sisters Denny and Chrissy for their unwavering love and support. Thanks to brother Mike for believing in me, and wishing that brother Hardy were here to see the book published. Thanks to Susan March for being my trusted partner in the Antics adventure. I would also like to thank Jackie Auris and Cathy Weiss for being my "readers" and giving me constructive feedback and ongoing support. Thanks to my many friends and colleagues at the Chester County Intermediate Unit for their confidence and support. I would also like to thank Catherine Faherty and Dr. Jed Baker for offering encouragement through the publishing process. A very special thanks goes out to all of the actors in the Antics program for all that they have taught me, and to their families for believing so strongly in the program.

Thanks to Shaan Pickett for sharing his talent by doing the illustrations for the book. Shaan is a 16-year-old artist and Antics actor who lives with his family in West Chester, Pennsylvania.

Contents

Figures

Foreword

People who have Asperger Syndrome can be natural actors. Cindy Schneider has developed a manual to capitalize on the ability of children and adolescents with Asperger Syndrome to observe and copy gestures, tone of voice and mannerisms to teach social understanding and flexible thinking. The activities are based on her extensive experience as a teacher and autism consultant. Cindy also has a thorough understanding of the theoretical models of Asperger Syndrome and current research and how this knowledge can be applied to drama activities.

This book will be particularly helpful for teenagers with Asperger Syndrome who can be reluctant to participate in programs that imply the participants have a social disability, due to a fear of the contemptuous comments of peers. Participating in a drama group and having the ability to act can be admired by peers, and the dramatic arts perceived as "cool".

Acting Antics provides teachers, parents and therapists with an easy-to-read manual that provides advice on scenes, themes and scripts, the management of group dynamics and suggestions for equipment, costumes and props. The drama program is entertaining and informative for the participants and the audience, and can be integrated into a classroom curriculum or therapy session.

The best way to learn is by having fun, and *Acting Antics* will encourage people with Asperger Syndrome to act and enable them to react in everyday situations. They will be helped to develop a greater maturity in understanding what someone may be thinking or feeling and to communicate their own thoughts and feelings. *Acting Antics* will be essential reading for teachers, therapists and parents who want to know how to improve social understanding.

Professor Tony Attwood

Preface

The Thespian

When my sisters and I were young children, my mother enrolled us in a local children's theater program. It was to be run by a woman from our church, and held in the woman's backyard. My parents thought it would be a nice amusement for the summer. Little did they know that our director, Marilyn Gerold, had been a child star on Broadway, and was one of the most talented people I have ever met! Not only was she an amazing director, but she wrote all of the dialogue, lyrics and music for the shows. The scripts were wonderful versions of the traditional stories such as "Pinocchio," "Cinderella," "The Gingerbread House," etc. The characters she created were anything but traditional. They were bigger than life, and full of warmth and humor.

We rehearsed on her flagstone patio, as she ran to and from the piano, plunking out the tune and teaching us dance moves simultaneously. Everything about Marilyn's personality was big. Her voice was loud, her gestures were huge, and her ability to reach children was enormous. We had so much fun and learned so much during those summers. The time of our first big performance was fast approaching. We sang and moved and sang and moved some more. A week before show time an incredible array of costumes arrived from a New York costume house. Then, two days before our show, we arrived to see professional artists from New York painting our scenery. The next day, the day before our performance, a six-piece professional orchestra was warming up near the patio. Marilyn had called in all of her friends and colleagues to make our show a gala production!

Needless to say, my parents were stunned when they came to see the show on this little backyard patio. Not only were the production values amazing, but Marilyn had pulled unbelievable talent out of her troupe of local children.

I worked with Marilyn from the time I was about ten years old, right through my sophomore year of college when home on vacations. Herein lies the beginning of my lifelong passion for drama. Marilyn passed away a few years ago, but her influence on me and on many others will live forever.

Having now been bitten by the theater bug, I joined a community theater right out of college. It was there in fact that I met my best buddy and husband of 29 years. Initially an actor, I soon tried my hand at directing. By the time my boys were five and seven, I began directing the children's theater program, a venture that lasted 20 years. Each summer our troupe took a much-anticipated trip to perform at a camp for special needs children. This was a very special performance for our actors. After the performance the actors brought campers onstage to try on costumes and sing some of the songs from the show. Afterwards our actors toured the facility, and then joined the campers for a picnic lunch. When we returned to the theater, the actors would share experiences. A discussion about our own similarities and differences ensued. Actors shared experiences of feeling "different" because of personal issues. One actor shared that he had Attention Deficit Disorder (ADD), and would become frustrated because people got impatient with him. A young lady with a growth hormone disorder shared what it was like always to be treated as a smaller child when she was on the cusp of the teenage years. As a group the actors discussed ways that they could help to encourage the celebration of differences in their circles of friends and family.

Our lessons in acceptance were put to the test as we began to have youngsters with a variety of abilities join our troupe. One year we had two boys diagnosed with Asperger Syndrome (AS), one diagnosed with Autism, three youngsters with Attention Deficit Hyperactivity Disorder (ADHD), a very young girl with juvenile diabetes, and a young girl with a hearing aid. Indeed my young actors, all 36 of them, put into practice what they had discussed, and every actor was fully accepted as a vital member of our troupe.

The professional

A classroom special educator for 20 years, as students diagnosed with Autism were enrolled in my class, I became fascinated with this diagnosis and the unique individuals who fall under that umbrella. Autism and Asperger Syndrome became the focus of my professional development and personal research. Autism Spectrum Disorders, and the families affected by them, became my professional passion.

After 20 years in the classroom, I became an Autism Consultant, offering training and support regarding students with Autism Spectrum Disorders to teachers throughout our county. This position gave me the opportunity to interact with teachers, students, and parents dealing with issues all along the Autism continuum. While the amazing students diagnosed with Asperger Syndrome more and more intrigued me, the lack of effective programming being implemented to teach social understanding to these students quickly became apparent.

Putting it together

Students diagnosed with Asperger Syndrome, or other social cognition deficits, lack the understanding of nonverbal communication that so many of us take for granted. A nod of the head, a smirk, a change in voice tone, are so often misinterpreted or totally missed by those with this deficit. Enter "Acting". What is acting all about? It is about reading and portraying emotions by using your voice as well as nonverbal communication. It is about acting and reacting. It is about developing a relationship with other actors onstage. It is about interpreting the language of a script. Is that not a perfect match? Hence, four years ago, I began this journey, combining my personal and professional passions to create theater programs for these students. It has been an incredibly satisfying endeavor, and one that makes me want to shout from the rooftops, "Try this! They'll love it!" So now I share this with you, parents and professionals, in the hope that some of you will pick up the reins and initiate your own programs.

This book is intended to be a "how-to" manual for starting your own drama group with youngsters who have social cognition deficits. Clearly this is meant to be a guideline. Hopefully, once you start a group you will alter, delete and add things to make it your own! You do not need to have extensive acting experience to do this program. What you do need is an understanding of the areas of social deficits, and the willingness to jump in enthusiastically! You want to teach the actors to take risks in trying new things, so clearly you need to be willing to do that as well. I hope that some of the anecdotes which you will read along the way will demonstrate the effect that acting activities can have on the lives of our students with AS.

Chapter 1

Introduction

Carl

It was Wednesday of a week-long theater camp for young students diagnosed with Asperger Syndrome. We were learning very simple movements to a song that was to be our "finale" in our Friday showcase. The lyrics spoke about the show being over and thanks for coming and so on. I looked up and one of my little guys, six-year-old Carl, had tears in his eyes. When I asked what was wrong he burst into sobs and said, "I don't want it to be over!"

Before beginning the discussion of the specifics of using theater as a social tool for youngsters diagnosed with social cognition deficits, it is important to identify what those deficits include. Students with Asperger Syndrome (AS) are those who developed significant language skills by the age of five. They had substantial spoken vocabularies and age-appropriate syntax. These youngsters, however, have difficulty with the *reciprocal* nature of communication, or the give and take of conversation. Their language can tend to be more like giving a speech than having a conversation.

Michelle Garcia Winner is the Director of the Center for Social Thinking in San Jose, California. Her work is focused on teaching social cognition to youngsters who have diagnoses including AS and nonverbal learning disability. Winner discusses distinct deficits caused by overlapping learning disabilities in these individuals. These include conceptual, inferential, language formulation and per-spective-taking learning disabilities (Winner 2002, p.x).

A *conceptual learning disability* refers to deficits in concept formation, or "big picture" thinking. Persons diagnosed with AS tend to be detail oriented at the expense of the broader view. This can lead to difficulty with problem solving, and prioritizing. Consider the following scenario:

> John has been asked to summarize the chapter for the class. John begins to expound on every event that occurred in the chapter (lack of "big picture" thinking). After five minutes his classmates are beginning to shift in their seats and roll their eyes, and the teacher begins looking at her watch. John keeps talking (does not read nonverbal communicative signals). When finished the middle school class begins to clap mockingly. John thinks they are clapping because he has done a good job (not understanding what or how others think). On the playground the boys start teasing him about talking too much and laugh at him. John does not understand.

John could remember and recount details, but could not synthesize information into a summary. This same disability prevents many students from being able to discern the "main idea" of a paragraph.

Additionally, these students have difficulties in "executive function". Our executive functioning allows us to sequence, prioritize, shift attention, and generally organize ourselves. This skill set is functioning automatically in most of us who are neurologically intact. In individuals diagnosed with AS, the frontal lobe of the brain has differences causing the executive function deficit. Consequently, they have great difficulty planning, organizing, or shifting attention. This deficit also makes multitasking a problem (Myles and Adreon 2001, p.10). These deficits can cause obvious difficulty in academics, but also have major ramifications for all aspects of life. As adults, most of us plan, organize, make adjustments to the plan, and add something new to the plan, all without a second thought. In the middle of the planning we answer the telephone, help a child blow his nose, let the dog out, respond to a colleague, all without missing a beat. This planning and shifting is something individuals with AS must explicitly be taught.

An *inferential learning disability* can be seen in the individual's difficulty with abstract language, implied meaning, and figurative language. A deficit in the ability to infer also creates difficulty in understanding nonverbal communication signals (Winner 2002). If the individual does not read those nonverbal signals, he is unlikely to be able to use them in his own communication. Imagine what it would be like if you did not read nonverbal language. Think about the last staff meeting, parent–teacher organization (PTO) meeting, club meeting, individual education plan (IEP) meeting, or family dinner you have attended. What nonverbal signals were being given that may not have been heard anywhere in the dialogue? In what positions were people seated? Did that hold meaning? How did people respond when different people spoke? Could you tell who was well liked and who was not? Did anyone roll his eyes at a particular point? Did anyone look bored? Did anyone keep checking her watch? Now imagine if you did not know how to read any of those signals. And imagine that you were also totally unaware of what signals you were or were not giving.

A *language formation disability* is evidenced in a difficulty formulating and initiating language in a reciprocal conversation (Winner 2002). A person diagnosed with AS often would rather do a monologue about his favorite subject. This individual may show no interest at all in what the other person might say, but may direct the conversation back to his favorite subject. Youngsters with AS often interact more comfortably with adults, and adults will sometimes report that the individual is a competent communicator. Indeed, the youngster may have a tremendous vocabulary and can speak volumes about whatever he is interested in. What the adult may fail to realize is how much he or she has compensated for the youngster's communication deficits. Adults are much more willing to tolerate a conversation on a topic of little interest to them. Adults are also more likely to provide ample processing time by waiting patiently. They may even tolerate the youngster's unwillingness to change topics (Myles and Adreon 2001, p.16).

This deficit also creates difficulty for the individual in using language to problem solve. Problem solving requires may language-based steps. First a person needs to identify the problem. Next a person may need to come up with alternative solutions to the problem. Then one needs to analyze and predict what the possible outcomes of each solution might be. Next an alternative solution must be chosen and implemented. For an individual who has a disability in the area of language formation, this process would be overwhelming.

Perhaps one of the areas of greatest impact is the *perspective-taking learning disability*. This is often referred to as a deficit in Theory of Mind (Baron-Cohen and Bolton 1993, p.46). Theory of Mind has been described as an awareness of what others think or know. After children reach the age of about four, they begin to understand that other people have thoughts and feelings different from their own (Attwood 1998, p.112). The ability to predict what these thoughts or feelings might be continues to grow as children develop. Winner characterizes this skill as making "smart guesses" (Winner 2002, p.32). When this skill is lacking, a person can easily say things that hurt the feelings of another. Think of the three-year-old who tells Aunt Matilda that her breath stinks. Since individuals with AS often lack the ability to make "smart guesses" about what another person thinks and feels, they often say just what is on their mind, just as the three-year-old in the earlier example. They do not intend to be cruel or hurt the other person's feelings; they simply do not know how to take another's perspective. A person who cannot make "smart guesses" about what another may think or feel often appears rude and self-centered. In a sense they are self-centered, not because they choose to be but because their social deficits do not allow them to see past their own thoughts and feelings.

When one does not have this perspective-taking skill, it is also difficult to determine the needs or intentions of others. It is therefore difficult to determine how others might expect you to think or behave in different situations. This also creates individuals at risk of being taken advantage of by those with negative motives or intentions. Here is another true illustration of a social deficit in this area:

> Fred is very "typical" in his appearance. Fred has very recently been diagnosed with AS. Fred is at lunch with his peers. He wants very much to be a part of the group, but is usually just on the periphery. Fred's peers tell him it would be very funny if he said "_____" to a girl at the neighboring table. Fred leans over and does this. The girl and her friends look very upset, but the boys are laughing. Fred laughs and feels good to be part of the group. When Fred reports to his next class he is sent to the office where he meets with a very angry principal who accuses him of sexual harassment.

As a result of this incident, staff and peers instantly labeled Fred as a "pervert." The special educator who understood Fred's recent diagnosis worked hard to quickly do damage control, explaining the diagnosis and deficits to the teaching staff. However, reputations are very difficult to repair. Fred's inability to understand the motives of others had a significant negative impact on his high school experience.

As you can see, the youngsters who are dealing with this diagnosis often have social deficits that significantly impact on their lives. Because they often are bright and quite verbal, their disability is a hidden one and they are often misunderstood and mistreated by peers and sometimes by adults. Low self-esteem becomes a huge issue for these youngsters, particularly as they approach middle school years. We must do a better job of teaching these youngsters how to understand other people so they are better equipped to function successfully in society.

There are a number of wonderful resources and programs for teaching youngsters about social understanding, rather than simply "social skills". Carol Gray is one of the pioneers in the field with her work regarding Social Stories™ and Comic Strip Conversations. Social Stories™ are individualized stories written at the child's instructional level to help him or her better understand a social situation (Gray 1998, p.6). This is a strategy that has been taught and employed worldwide with significant success.

Michelle Garcia Winner has developed the "I LAUGH" approach in her book entitled *Inside Out: What Makes a Person with Social Cognitive Deficits Tick?* (Winner 2000). She goes on to further explore social understanding in her next book, *Thinking About You Thinking About Me*. Winner looks very closely at the different deficits and how they affect the individual in social situations. Her focus is on teaching students to be "social detectives" (Winner 2002, p.32).

Brenda Smith Myles and colleagues have provided a great perspective in their book entitled *The Hidden Curriculum*. They define the hidden curriculum as the rules or guidelines in a situation that are not directly taught, but rather are assumed (Myles, Trautman, and Schelvan 2004). The authors indicate that you are probably referring to a hidden curriculum item when you say any of the following:

- I shouldn't have to tell you, but…

- It should be obvious that…

- Everyone knows that…

- Common sense tells us…

- No one ever… (Myles *et al.* 2004, p.5)

These unwritten rules include what to wear, how to act, what to say and not say in a variety of settings. Additionally, the hidden curriculum changes from one setting to the next, and with adolescents from one fad to the next!

Jed Baker has written an entire curriculum of practical lessons in his book entitled *Social Skills Training for Children and Adolescents with Asperger Syndrome and Social Communication Problems*. Dr. Baker wisely writes the following in his Introduction:

> From a parent's or educator's perspective, a crucial goal of a social skills group is that children will learn social skills that will help them gain greater acceptance. However, from the group member's point of view, having and being with friends in the group may be the most important issue, regardless of any skills learned. With this in mind, an effective group cannot just be a class, but must be a place where members feel safe and enjoy themselves. (Baker 2003, p.7)

These and other resources are listed in the References list at the back of the book. I highly recommend these resources for more in-depth discussion of the social cognition deficits of individuals diagnosed with AS, and practical strategies to address those deficits.

This book, however, is intended to take a different approach to addressing these deficits. In drama, understanding concepts, making and interpreting inferences, taking another's perspective, and formulating language are all key components in working on a scene. You will notice as you proceed through the manual that these components are addressed in a variety of activities in the Acting Antics program. As a quick reminder, there will be "Key skills" that will be noted for different activities. These will be easily recognizable because they will be labeled like this. Do not hesitate to return to Chapter 1 as needed to refresh your understanding of the skill deficits.

Key skills

✓
✓
✓

Chapter 2

Who? What? Where?

Amy

Amy loved to perform. She had auditioned for a show at her school and had not been cast. When telling me about this she was very aware that the director double-cast the show, casting two actors for every role. "And I still didn't get a part!" she exclaimed. She participated in our group with great enthusiasm. After the show she waved her arm in the air saying, "I'd better go say goodbye to my adoring fans!" And off she went to the lobby where her fans were waiting.

The Acting Antics program lends itself to a great deal of flexibility in terms of how and where the activities can be done. In this chapter the reader will learn how these techniques can be used in a variety of settings, and by a range of adults working with youngsters.

If you have not been involved in drama before and you are now saying, "But I am not an actor! I can't do this," or "I have a whole classroom of students—I can't do this," or "I have IEP objectives to meet in therapy sessions—I can't do this!", I say to you, "Yes, yes, yes, you certainly can!"

In the home

Families can effectively use many of the activities outlined in this manual in the home. They are designed to teach children social understanding while providing vibrant and fun activities for the family. Some, such as "Bamboozle" (Chapter 3), "Open Scenes" (Chapter 4), and "Partner Scenes" (Chapter 5) are very appropriate to use with only two or three people. Others, such as "Energy Circle" (Chapter 3), "Larger Group Scenes" (Chapter 5), and "Slow News Day" (Chapter 6) might be more enjoyable with a small group of four or five people.

Many parents spend every day trying to think of new ways to help their children understand the social world in order to lessen their anxiety. Without even thinking about it, you constantly interpret environments, events, and emotions for your son or daughter, smoothing his or her way in a very unpredictable world. The Antics program is one more tool for the parent's bag of tricks! Read on with a sense of adventure and determination. It will be worth it!

If you can bring siblings into the mix, it can be a really fun family activity to schedule one evening a week. If your family is small, try pairing up with one or two other families. In no way do the other youngsters need to have a diagnosis; these activities are fun and build confidence for all! If your youngsters are reluctant at the beginning, be sure to offer an incentive, such as time to play video games afterward. My expectation is that after they have done a session or two, they will look forward to the activities. The key is to make it fun, and not the drudgery of "social skills" that they may have been exposed to previously. When I work with groups everything is done in the context of learning to be an actor. You could do the same in the home, or you could simply use the activities as family games.

Some of the activities lend themselves to larger groups. These include "Taxi Driver" and the game of "Freeze" (Chapter 6). You could pre-teach your youngster the skills involved, and then introduce the full activity when you have a larger group at hand. This might work for a family gathering, for example, and your youngster could teach the game. "Taxi Driver" is perfect for this. Reluctant adults have been called upon to try this game during my teaching seminars. After the first few nervous moments, they were laughing and fully participating. How great if your child could be the initiator of this kind of fun at your next family holiday gathering!

Introducing some of these activities to a group such as your child's scout group is another way to share the fun. Again, if your child has already learned the skill set, he or she can be very involved in the teaching of activities. I have yet to meet a group of youngsters who has not been engaged by these activities!

Another parent arranged to have a "theater" party for her 11-year-old son. The children who attended were neurotypical (NT), or without a diagnosis. The group did several of the activities including one of the "silly skits" (Appendix C). They all had a wonderful time, and the birthday boy was able to help lead because he had previous experience with the games.

As therapy

These techniques can be readily used to address many of the areas in which young people undergoing speech therapy, counseling or occupational therapy need assistance. Deficit areas covered include pragmatic language, proxemics, social language, nonverbal messages, problem solving, group interaction, organizational skills, spatial concepts, motor planning, and sequencing. Some activities, such as "Props" (Chapter 6), "Bamboozle" (Chapter 3), and "Flexible Phrases" (Chapter 4), could be effectively used with one or two students and the therapist. Partner activities (Chapter 4) and scripted scenes (Chapter 5) could be performed with the client and the therapist playing the roles. In addition, consider the possibility of putting two groups together, or possibly importing one or two young people who may not be clients. Often, adding young people to create a group atmosphere fosters excitement and full participation.

In my experience, the co-treatment model pairing speech clinicians and occupational therapists together has been very effective. No individual deficit area with our students exists in isolation. For example, a lack of spatial awareness is often a deficit in the social understanding piece, and also in the way the student's motor and sensory system is functioning. Co-treating with professionals from different disciplines allows for a broader application and generalization of skills. When professionals collaborate, seeing the youngsters in a common setting, the strategies that arise from this collaboration are likely to be implemented in more than one school environment. This implementation in multiple environments lays the groundwork for generalization of skills.

Having a larger group, even if only three or four students, creates the opportunity to utilize many more activities. It also allows for the client to work with other peers. Many of the young people we are targeting already perform better socially with adults than with peers! We want them to learn how to interact with their peers. If at all possible, include one or two NT young people, or young people who do not have a diagnosis and are socially able, in your group. If working in a school setting this can be arranged during study hall, or as a way to fulfill a service project. Employ these students not as "helpers," but as part of the acting group. These students can often be great role models in the group, and also are very helpful in demonstrating activities that might take the target students a bit longer to grasp. Partner the NT young person with someone who may be more impaired and might need more modeling, or perhaps with a young person who is less socially impaired who might be up to more of a challenge, dramatically speaking.

In school

Classroom teachers may not think they are actors, but performing is what they do all day long, until it has become second nature! They perform, they direct, they model, and they facilitate all day long. These are the same skills that will be used when implementing some of the Antics activities in the classroom.

A regular classroom educator who is reading this may be thinking, "How would I ever fit this into my day? With all of the demands on us for academic performance, can I afford to spend time on 'acting'? I only have two identified students in my room…can I justify spending time on this?"

These techniques can be used in so many different ways, and can benefit so many different students, in particular those students who:

- are extremely self-conscious when having to speak in front of the class

- do not articulate clearly

- speak entirely too softly

- speak too loudly much of the time

- exhibit inappropriate classroom posture or body language

- don't read nonverbal signals well

- are quick to argue and slow to problem solve or negotiate

- have difficulty working on a group project in class

- have difficulty with abstract language

- are bullied

- are bullies.

Regular classrooms today comprise a wide range of students with a wide range of needs. If we do not teach all of our youngsters appropriate social cognition skills, they will have difficulty becoming effective and fulfilled citizens. Many of these skill deficits can be addressed by using the Antics activities, regardless of whether or not a student has a diagnosis. For the child who does indeed have a diagnosis in which social cognition deficits are characteristic, it is our responsibility as educators to address these needs.

In elementary school, improvisation activities could be done as an indoor recess activity, a circle time activity, or even as part of a critical thinking or problem solving activity (see Chapter 6 for more information). Partner activities (Chapter 5) can be done as a culmination of a reading activity. An activity such as "Slow News

Day" (Chapter 6) can be a great cooperative group activity. The object or topic about which a group designs the news show could easily be content related. Now you not only have all of your students working on interaction and presentation skills, but you also have them reinforcing academic material.

Additionally, in the elementary classroom there often are occasions to address issues involving values clarification such as diversity, bullying and peer pressure. "Scenes from a Hat" (Chapter 6) is a fun and effective activity to teach students to begin to think about ways to problem solve. This activity allows for you to generate scenarios that are most relevant to your class's or your school's particular areas of concern.

In the high school environment, "Scenes from a Hat" could be taken to a new level, addressing decision-making skills and social issues. Additionally, many of the improvisational games can be very useful both for the social value and by integrating content material (see Chapter 6 for activities and application). Counselors and special educators could use theater activities as they run their social groups. Creating a theater or improvisation club during or after school would be a great way to use these activities. This club, unlike the big high school musical, would focus on the process of using these activities to hone acting skills. In order to make it really effective for the students we are targeting, the facilitator would need to be familiar with the social deficits involved, and which activities can help address those deficit areas.

Special education classrooms for socially challenged youngsters probably already involve some social instruction as part of the curriculum. This is a wonderful set-up for using many of the activities described in this book. Again, if possible, you would want to recruit a few "guest" actors from outside of the special education setting. If your schedule includes social skills instruction on two, three, or more days a week, perhaps certain sessions could be designated as theater days! Even if your opportunity to work with the group socially is only once a week, an effective program with structure and sequence can be set up, using the activities described in Chapters 4, 5 and 6.

In summary

Whether you are a parent, teacher, therapist, or otherwise, once you get involved in doing these activities, you may find that you are interested in starting a group on a regular basis. This undertaking would seem less daunting if you have made a connection with another parent or professional who believes in this approach and will help you in this endeavor. When you arrive at that point, Chapter 7, "Starting Your Own Troupe," provides step-by-step directions about how to navigate that exciting process. In the meantime, just begin by choosing one activity to use with your child or your students. And *have fun*, because that is the key to the success of this approach!

Chapter 3

Getting Started

Jay

It was the first session of one of our very first teen workshops. Parents and teens arrived, all somewhat nervous about how this would go. Many parents stayed around during the session, outside the auditorium in which we worked. At the end of the two-hour session, we opened the doors and the families were reunited. A father came up to me and said, "I don't know what you were doing in there, but I have never before experienced a situation in which my son was engaged and laughing with peers for a two-hour period! It was amazing!"

Breaking the ice

It is important to make the actors feel comfortable right away and let them know that this is going to be fun. Humor is a great way to accomplish both of those goals. Here is one way of doing that, while also beginning a conversation about nonverbal cues. Gather the actors in a circle, and then go out of the room and make an entrance. Stomp into the room, scowling and growling with arms crossed. Go to the group and then say in a low, grouchy and unconvincing voice, "I am so happy to see you all here today." If you want to be really dramatic, you can slam a folder down on something at the end of the "bit." Some students will be giggling, some will look at you like you should be taken away for medical intervention, and others will just have a stunned look. Then say to them, "Did you believe me?" They quickly say,

"NO." This is a great opportunity to elicit from them what specific things belied your words. Soon you have established what will be called "The Big 3." These are:

1. Vocal tone and volume.

2. Body language.

3. Facial expression (see Figure 3.1).

Key skills

✓ Introduction of "The Big 3"
✓ Understanding humor
✓ Building a comfort level in group

The "Big 3" will be the cornerstone of much of our work in the coming sessions. After you have established "The Big 3," ask the group if you could re-enter, say the same words, but now change "The Big 3," and be believable. They will probably be anxious to tell you how this could be done. At this point you can either demonstrate, or have one of the actors demonstrate, a more positive entrance. Review the changes in "The Big 3" that made it believable the second time.

The Big 3

1. Vocal tone

2. Body language

3. Facial expression

Figure 3.1 The Big 3

Warming up

It is important now to have the actors begin to work in a group, be successful, and have fun. Activities done standing in a circle are good warm-ups and non-threatening. First, each participant (this always includes any helpers) shares one or two things he or she would like the group to know about him or her. With younger groups you may need to be very specific by saying something such as "two things you like to do." One young actor answered, for example, "My name is John and I like video games and cartooning." During this activity with a teenage group, one boy said, "My name is _____, I like to draw and I have Asperger Syndrome." The next young man said, "I have Asperger Syndrome, too. Nice to meet you!" Suddenly it almost sounded like a badge of honor! How wonderful!

This next activity is designed to get the class or small group of students warmed up by physically moving. A teacher/colleague/actor taught me this activity. "Shake It Up" is done in circle or line formation. The leader raises one arm and shakes it eight times, counting aloud as she shakes. Next, put that arm down, raise the other arm and shake it eight times, counting aloud. Do the same with each foot, counting to eight each time. Now start with the arm again, this time counting to seven. Do a count of seven with both arms and then legs. Repeat counting to six. Start this at a fairly relaxed pace, but gradually speed it up so that by the time you get to "one" everyone will be frantic and laughing as they try to keep pace. Give different actors the opportunity to lead the activity.

Stretching activities are also beneficial. As the actors do different stretches you can have them make silly sounds as well. This can warm up the vocal chords as well as encouraging the actor to begin "taking risks" by being silly. These warm-ups are fun to use in a family group as well as in a more structured situation.

"Name Game"

Another game we will play is something called the "Name Game." If the members of the group are meeting for the first time, or have several new members, wearing nametags is suggested. This is played in a circle formation. One person starts by clapping his or her hands one time in the direction of another person across the circle and saying his or her name. It is important for the clapper to lean in towards that person, extend arms to clap toward the other actor, and to look at him or her. Next, the receiver of the clap looks and claps one time to another person in the circle, saying that person's name, and so on. The goal in this game is threefold:

- to get the actors physically engaged and get their blood flowing

- to have them begin to learn one another's names if there are new members in the group

- to begin working on the nonverbal skills of body position and looking at the listener.

Eventually try to speed up the game to work on the actors' response time.

It is important in the "Name Game" that *everyone* be successful. If there is someone who wants just to observe at first, certainly let them do that. If there is someone who does not read the names quickly, quietly assist. It is rare not to have everyone engaged by the end of the first trial of the game.

Key skills

✓ Attending to others
✓ Learning the names of peers
✓ Learning how to look for signals from others
✓ Improving response time
✓ Experiencing success

After the first run of the "Name Game," if you have members in the group who are new to you, have the actors cover their nametags and try to say all of the names. They love it when you make a mistake! This is something else we want to teach them, right? Making a mistake is OK? So run with it! The next day you might close your eyes and have them all change places in the circle. Then when you open your eyes, act like you are totally confused. You might call some of them outrageous names (you will know by now who will tolerate that) before you finally get it right. As the week goes on, begin to ask if there is anyone who thinks they can name three fellow actors when the nametags are covered. Several usually volunteer, and you are likely to get the one who already knows all of the names. Ideally by the end of the week you will not need the nametags and everyone will know the names of the other actors. Sometimes that is the case, sometimes not.

"Energy Circle" or "The Power"

"Energy Circle" was renamed by one of my teenage groups to "The Power" and you will soon see why. Again done in the circle, this time the single clap simply gets passed around the circle, either to the left or the right. Each person turns to his neighbor and claps once in his direction, then the neighbor turns to the next person and claps, and so on. The idea is to do it somewhat rapidly, all in the same direction initially, creating a wave-like effect. The fun comes when one person (the leader initially) has the power to change directions. When the clap gets to you, you have the power to clap back to the person who clapped to you, sending the wave in the opposite direction. Eventually, assign someone on the other side of the circle also to have the power, so that the direction can change in two different locations. As the group gets better at this, you can add a third and even a fourth person that has the power, and watch the fun as the clap gets stuck going back and forth in a small section of the circle!

Not only is this game a great deal of fun for the actors, but it has many wonderful skills embedded in it. First, and perhaps most importantly, the actors must *focus*, because it moves quickly and you must be paying attention in order to maintain the movement around the circle. Once again this is also a great exercise for improving response time, as it can move along at a good pace. Next, it is a great way to work on "shifting," or changing tracks. You think that the clap is going to go one way, and suddenly you need to turn and send it back the other way. For some students, that is difficult initially. You will see right away if you need to stand near one of the actors to provide an additional cue. This is also a place to use your NT actors. You can have them discreetly stand beside someone who might need a prompt.

"Bamboozle"

Whereas the "Name Game" and "Energy Circle" are best played with groups of four or more, "Bamboozle" can easily be played with as few as one youngster and one adult.

The word "bamboozle" was chosen for this activity because it had three syllables that seemed to work well. However, this past year one of the groups suggested using "Spongebob Squarepants," and that has stuck, at least for now.

In "Bamboozle," start with a list of words that express how a person feels (see Boxes 3.1 and 3.2). The director recites one of the words to the actor, and he or she is to show the meaning of that "feeling" word by using the "Big 3":

1. Vocal tone and volume.

2. Body language.

3. Facial expression (refer back to Figure 3.1).

The actor is to portray that feeling while saying the designated phrase "Bamboozle." (You may need to read this paragraph again!) Example: You, the leader, say the word "confused" to the first actor. The actor then says "Bamboozle" as if he or she is confused. This might include scrunching up the face, looking upward, shrugging shoulders, and having intonation rise at the end of the phrase as if in a question. For groups of four or more, "Bamboozle" can be played while the actors are in the circle. Each actor around the circle gets a new word assigned by the director, and on his or her turn says the designated phrase while portraying the

Box 3.1 Feeling words, level 1

happy	frustrated	confused
sad	noisy	excited
sleepy	angry	silly
freezing	scared	quiet
shy	cool	dizzy
itchy	surprised	bratty

Box 3.2 Feeling words, level 2

goofy	happy	intelligent
confused	sad	sleepy
hilarious	angry	itchy
catty	frustrated	impatient
obnoxious	tired	distracted
amazed	hot	nervous
disappointed	silly	embarrassed
devious	cool	clumsy
alert	snobby	bossy
daydreaming	bratty	painful
paranoid	frightened	annoyed
flirtatious	surprised	cocky
sweet	stupid	shy
sour	freezing	tough
mean	thirsty	excited
playful	hungry	gross
tiny	dizzy	peaceful
huge	fabulous	insulted
tight	worried	gorgeous

assigned feeling, using the "Big 3." You may find it is easiest to have the written list of feeling words from which to choose. By now you have gotten somewhat of a feel for the abilities of your students, and can assign more difficult feelings to the more capable students (see Box 3.1 and 3.2 for two differentiated word lists). Another variation is to have one of your actors assign the feeling words from your list.

Keep in mind that the entire circle activity time should only be about 15 to 20 minutes, depending also on the length of your session, so you are probably not going to do all of these every day. You will soon find which ones your group particularly likes and which ones you feel are most beneficial. Alternating games on different days keeps things from becoming stagnant. With a smaller family or therapy group, your session might consist entirely of one or two of these activities.

The rules of acting

Once you have gotten the students on board with some fun activities, it is important to discuss the expectations for your group. Two basic rules have emerged as the ones that cover it all. The first is: *Never hurt an actor.* Discuss what it means not to hurt another actor. Some of your youngsters may be very anxious to tell you about stunt men and computer graphics in movies. Talk about how fighting is done onstage and in movies so that no one gets hurt. But then try to elicit other ways that an actor could be hurt. Someone eventually talks about hurting someone's feelings, and that sparks further discussion. In the theater class, the actors are also going to be audience as their fellow actors rehearse the different scenes and activities. This is actually a very important part of what we will be doing. The actors as audience members will be asked to interpret body language, vocal delivery, and meaning. Talk about how to make *helpful, constructive* comments. Discuss the fact that actors do not always agree with each other on exactly how something should be delivered, and that that is OK.

That is a good segue into the second rule: *Listen to the director.* Ask the actors what would happen on a movie set if everybody did just exactly what they wanted,

Actor's Rules

1. Never hurt an actor

2. Listen to the director

Figure 3.2 Rules of acting

said their lines whenever they wanted, wore any costume they wanted. They are pretty quick to say that it would be a big confusing mess, so the director rule is a fairly easy sell. In some groups the actors chose to make a poster of the two rules and posted them in the room so that they were visible at all times (see Figure 3.2 and Appendix B).

Whether you are working with a larger theater class or with two youngsters in a family setting, teaching these rules is an important component. These rules are great ways to practice respecting others, and following direction from those in charge.

Terminology

There are two other acting terms you may want to teach the group. The first is to *cheat out*. This means to keep your body at an angle as you speak to another actor so that the audience can see you. It helps to give actors a specific corner of the room as a marker. "When you are on right stage, stand so your toes are pointing to the exit sign in the back left corner." This is very hard for some young actors and they will need reminding.

Another term is *project*, said with a long "o" sound. Direct the actors to project their voices out against the back wall, much like a projector throws its image out against the screen (of course with DVD and digital, projectors are practically obsolete now). Read a line from a scene first mumbling quietly. Then read the line again, *projecting* your voice clearly. Exaggerate, of course, to make the point. Ask the actors which delivery will better keep the audience's attention.

These issues are important not only to acting, but also to the work we are trying to do on the perspective-taking skills of the actors. When working in theater, it is always important to think about how the audience will perceive our performance. This begins with very basic questions: "Can they hear me?" "Can they see me?" Only after we have established those two basics can we broach questions such as "Will they think this is funny?" or "Will they like this character?" This is a great theatrical introduction to the skill of thinking about the perspective of others.

Key skills

✓ Responding to rules and structure
✓ Thinking about audience perspective
✓ Using visual supports
✓ Making visual supports

Make it visual

This may be a good place in which to emphasize the use of visual supports for your actors. Visualize the rules as shown above, but also cues such as "Cheat out" and "Project" as shown in sample posters in Figure 3.3 and Appendix B. They should be fun and user-friendly. Ideally, the actors can design and make these posters so that they have more of an investment in the concepts.

But posters won't be the only visuals you will want to use. You may want to use colored masking tape markings on the floor to help the actors know where to stand. You will probably want to make checklists for props, costumes, the order of scenes, etc. for backstage use. The functional use of a checklist may be one of the most significant lifelong strategies a student with AS can learn. If you can teach it in this fun environment, and help our actors see the value it, kudos to you!

Figure 3.3 Posters

Chapter 4

Paired Activities

Alex

A mom escorted a very reluctant 15-year-old Alex into the first weekly session. He told me he hated acting, did not want to be here, that it was baby stuff and there was no way he was going to participate. I told him that it was fine to sit back and just watch what was going on and I would check in with him later. We proceeded with our opening activities, and eventually into our group work. After at least a half hour I checked in and he still did not want to take part. He lay down and acted as though he was sleeping the rest of the session. Another teen diagnosed with AS took the initiative to gently approach him, but he received the same response.

At the end of the session, Alex's mom had not arrived by the time all of the other actors had been picked up. He paced a while telling me again how he hated acting. I asked him what he did like to do. He told me he liked television and hiking. When asked he told me some places where he had gone hiking, and came over to sit on the stage with me. Soon the conversation turned to his family, and he began to tell me about some of the significant stressors going on in his life. He was very angry with his sister, was worried about his mother, and so on and so on. Suddenly his entire demeanor changed; he clearly needed an ear to listen to his very real anxieties. By the end of the 15-minute conversation, I mentioned to Alex that I had a short scene about hiking (how's that for a stroke of good fortune?!), and I wondered if he would like to look at it. He said yes, and we read through it together. He seemed to respond well, so I suggested he take it home and read it again, and he could decide next week if he would like to act it out with two other actors. He agreed to think it over. His mom then came in and was very apologetic about being late. There had been some miscommunication about who was picking him up. I told her it had worked out well because Alex and I had gotten a chance to get to know each other, at which Alex smiled broadly.

Alex did perform the scene the next week, and in the showcase. In fact, he is one of those youngsters who really has a bit of a feel for line delivery. He has now attended three different sessions, as well as the Extended School Year camp program, and asks each time when the next one will be.

The following activities are designed to reinforce work on the "Big 3," as well as to facilitate each student's ability to work with others. It is best to begin with a short activity, so you can do a quick evaluation of how each actor responds in the paired situation. This will give you helpful information in terms of pairing actors for future activities.

Inanimate objects pantomime

This is a fun paired activity to use early in the sessions. Pairs or triads choose a card from a hat. On this card there is a word and/or picture of an inanimate object (e.g. bicycle, Christmas tree, popcorn, etc.). The team's assignment is to work together to create a charade in order to portray their object to the audience. The teams may *not* make sounds, and must portray the object itself, not someone using the object (they need to be the tree, not someone decorating it). For example, one group portrayed a Christmas tree in the following way. The tallest person stood behind the other two, who stood side by side. The taller actor in the back extended the fingers of his hands and placed both hands above his head, giving the suggestion of a star. The actors on the sides opened and closed their hands in an effort to portray blinking lights (see Figure 4.1).

This activity can not only be readily done in therapy sessions or at home, but might also be a creative way to have students demonstrate more abstract concepts in a concrete manner. In a unit on the cycle of a cell in science class, students could physically demonstrate the phases of mitosis, for example. In vocabulary lessons, students could work together to portray terminology in pantomime style. This type of activity utilizes whole body learning and peer interaction while focusing on academic material.

Fingers extended
to suggest a star

Hands opening and closing
to indicate
blinking lights

Figure 4.1 Christmas tree

"Flexible Phrases"

In "Flexible Phrases," short phrases are written on strips of paper or cardstock. Laminating the phrases is recommended so that you do not have to re-create them for each session. The group is divided into pairs; more significantly socially impaired youngsters should initially be paired with your NT actors. If there is an uneven number you can create a group of three, or pair an adult with one of the actors. Each group is given a strip of paper on which a phrase is written (example: "Look at this"). The pair is to determine two different emotions with which the phrase could be delivered, and how it would be said in each case. Actors are asked to remember the "Big 3" while working on this. Adults circulate and help as needed (see Box 4.1 for an example).

Key skills

✓ Working in a group
✓ Expressing using nonverbals
✓ Reading or interpreting nonverbal signals

"Flexible Phrases" is an activity you may want to revisit several times during the subsequent sessions, assigning new phrases and using different pairings of actors. Some of the actors will grasp this concept pretty quickly, but for others it is a significant challenge. Some youngsters with AS have a really tough time hearing the vocal differences in line delivery. These actors might have difficulty hearing that the emphasis was on a particular word, or that the phrase went up at the end as in a question. For these actors you may need to model the desired delivery, and then give visual cues for how you want them to deliver the line. You can even use visual cues for speed of delivery and for volume (see Box 4.2 for examples).

Box 4.1 "Flexible Phrases" examples

| **Example A:** | Mom is looking at a muddy footprint on the carpet, and says, "Look at this." |
| **Example B:** | Pete has just downloaded an awesome new video game he wants to show his brother and says, "Look at this." |

Box 4.2 Ways of using "Flexible Phrases"

"What was that?"	(simple, direct question)
"WHAT…WAS…**THAT?**"	(frightened of "that")
"What was **THAT?**"	(annoyance—the other person has just done something inappropriate)
"I'm not going."	(matter of fact)
"**I'm** not going."	(you might be, but **I'm** not)
"I'm **NOT** going!"	(you can't convince me to go)

One of the important components of this activity is having each pair "perform" the lines for the rest of the group. As audience members, the youngsters are asked to interpret the meaning of the line as delivered by the actor. During this interpretation, it is not adequate that an audience person says "because he sounded angry." He or she will then be asked specifically what made the actor sound angry. Did he speak loudly or softly? Quickly or slowly? Is there a word that was emphasized? What was his face doing? What was his body doing? How was this different from how his partner said the same phrase? It is important that actors come away from this activity understanding that the way the line is delivered is what ultimately creates the meaning.

Key skills

✓ Understanding the perspective of others
✓ Understanding the meaning of nonverbal signals

For the youngsters with whom you are working one of the biggest social issues is the deficit in the area of Theory of Mind (Baron-Cohen and Bolton 1993, pp.46–47). This deficit makes it difficult for these youngsters to take the perspective of another person. Therefore, they do not have an understanding of how others interpret what they say or do. "Flexible Phrases" is an activity in which we start to explore how what we say, and even more importantly, how we say it, is interpreted by others.

This is an activity that is also very conducive to use in a smaller family or therapy setting as well. Once you have introduced the concept, you may hear phrases in the environment that you want to bring into the game.

> *Scenario*: You and your youngster are in a restaurant and you overhear someone say, "Can I have some ketchup please?" to the server. The tone and body language suggest that this is more of an unpleasant demand than a polite request. The server turns away, frowns and sighs. You discreetly point this out and interpret the body language while dining.

When you return home, you can replay this incident, interpreting the nonverbal language of both parties. How was the "Big 3" used by the diner and by the server? Might the server's reaction have been different if the diner's "Big 3" had been different? Replay again using different nonverbal cues this time.

"Open Scenes"

"Open Scenes" are an extension of the "Flexible Phrases" activity. These scenes are for two actors and comprise four lines. The four lines are written so that they can have more than one interpretation (see Box 4.3 for an example).

In the first reading of these lines, scenario #1, actors are told that the two boys are talking about going to the Grand Opening of a new arcade in town. They are very excited to go. In the second reading, scenario #2, the boys have to go with their parents to a boring event at their school. Neither wants to go, so the lines are now said with boredom and some sarcasm. Sarcasm is an important concept for the actors to understand, especially the teens, because they will encounter it in a lot of

---

Box 4.3 Open scene

John: Are you going tonight?

Ed: Yeah, I can't wait.

John: Should be lots of fun.

Ed: Yeah, right.

---

real life situations. Since the youngsters with AS are very literal, the concept of saying exactly what you *don't* mean is sometimes a foreign one to them.

Depending on the ages and abilities of your actors, this activity can be presented to them in a couple of different ways. For some actors, you will need to give them the specific scenarios, and help with the appropriate delivery of the lines. For others who are older and/or more capable, you can have *them* come up with the scenarios and delivery. Again this is a great activity for the actors in the audience now to do some analysis of the scenes. Facilitate discussion about how each pair of scenes has been performed. How did the actors portray two entirely different scenarios using the exact same words? This is where the director coaches the audience members to be very specific in their comments. See Box 4.4 for an example of the audience debriefing after the second scenario where the boys are bored and using sarcasm.

While working on this activity, it is very necessary for the adults to circulate among the groups to help the actors as they prepare two different readings of these scenes. You will see that is fairly easy for some of your actors, but very difficult for others. "Open Scenes" are great for really driving home the concept that your voice, body language, and facial expression are powerful communicators. A number of open scenes are given in Appendix C, and you are welcome to photocopy them, or adapt them in any way.

Pairing actors

Another directing issue is deciding how to pair the actors. At first you may want to pair someone more socially able with someone less socially able. However, it is also important for the more able actors to get an opportunity to work with one another, or with an NT actor, so they can really get the feel of doing a scene with someone who is more socially cognizant.

Box 4.4 Example of "debriefing" after open scene

Director:	How were John and Ed feeling the second time they did the scene?
Bill:	They were bored.
Director:	How did you know they were bored?
Bill:	They just looked, ya know…bored.
Director:	How did they show us that? Were they standing up straight and tall?
Bill:	No, they were kind of slouched.
Director:	OK, good. So their body language was kind of loose and slouched. [Director demonstrates.] And their faces?
Joe:	Bored.
Director:	And how did that show on their faces?
Joe:	Well…their heads were sort of down and they didn't smile or anything.
Amy:	They sounded bored too.
Director:	Good, how exactly did they sound?
Amy:	Y'know…bored.
Director:	Were they talking slowly or quickly?
Amy:	Slowly, and sort of dragged out.
Director:	OK, so sort of s-l-o-w and dragged o-u-t. Were their voices higher pitched or lower than in the first scene?
Jim:	Lower, definitely lower.
Director:	OK, so their voices were low and slow, and their bodies were slouched, and that told us they were bored. So why did Ed say he "couldn't wait" to go?
Amy:	He was being sarcastic.
Director:	OK, can anybody explain what sarcasm is?
	[and so on…]

Chapter 5

Scripted Partner and Group Scenes

Paul

Paul was a young actor who interacted with others to some degree in a very structured activity, but had great difficulty interacting socially. During our snack break he would often sit off by himself, entirely in his own world. During a week of summer camp for the younger actors, we introduced jokes as scripts for the first time. Paul loved it! He brought in a book of jokes the next day, and told jokes during snack time. Suddenly everyone was bringing in jokes, and Paul was totally involved in the socialization of the group.

Joke scripts

Jokes can provide exciting material for pairs of actors. Assign two-line jokes or riddles, or have the students come up with their own. The jokes should be simple and have two to four lines where possible. Have each pair do a series of three or four jokes. The pair needs to decide who says the first line, why the joke is funny, and how the actor should react when the punchline is delivered.

In Box 5.1 you will see a "joke card" that was designed for a pair of actors. In this case the jokes were grouped to have a related theme: animals. This is a great opportunity to look at a number of language concepts while having fun with the jokes. Many of these jokes are fraught with plays on words, double meanings, and language misinterpretations. Please believe me that you will need really to explain what some of these jokes mean to some of your actors! Once they get it though, you will see them bringing in new jokes, joke books, etc. Many of the youngsters really get into it.

Another way to work with jokes is to use a running script of two-person jokes. Then line the actors up randomly and have #1 and #2 actors come out to read the first joke. Then #1 leaves to get back in line and actor #3 comes out to read the next joke with #2. Then #2 exits to line up, and #4 does the next joke with #3, and so on. This has worked as a fun activity that requires the actor to follow the script carefully, so he or she can jump in when it is their turn. Each actor will work with a variety of partners, and deliver a different joke each time. This activity works on focus, the ability of the actor to shift, and understanding humor (see Figure 5.1 for a diagram of how this might work).

Box 5.1 Sample "joke script"

Joke 1

Scene	*A man is driving his car with two penguins on the backseat. A police officer stops him.*
Police officer:	Why don't you take those penguins to the zoo?
Man:	We went there yesterday. Today we're going to the movies.

Joke 2

Chris:	What should you do if your dog tries to eat your book?
John:	Take the words right out of his mouth!

Joke 3

Chris:	I'm sorry I ran over your cat.
John:	It's OK. I'll get another one.
Chris:	No, it's not OK. I'd like to replace your cat.
John:	All right. How good are you at catching mice?

Joke 4

Chris:	What do you see on the ground when it's raining cats and dogs?
John:	Poodles!

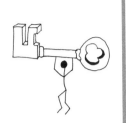

Key skills

✓ Shifting
✓ Being flexible
✓ Interpreting language
✓ Understanding humor

Actors 1 and 2 recite the first joke. Actor 1 exits to his left and returns to the back of the line. Actor 2 moves to the left position and actor 3 comes on to the right position. They recite next joke.

Actor 3 moves to left position and actor 4 moves to right position. They recite next joke. Pattern continues until all jokes are told.

Figure 5.1 Rotation for joke activity

"Partner Scenes"

In this activity, short two- or three-person scenes are assigned to groups of two or three. You will want to wait to assign scenes and partners until after the first session. This will give you an opportunity to get to know the students a bit so that you can choose partners effectively. Also, for this particular activity, the director needs to be sure to consider the reading level of each actor. For the actors that have a lower reading level, you can write or adapt scripts that require a minimum of reading. Also, an adult can prompt by modeling the line before the actor reads it. Take care never to have an actor feel self-conscious or embarrassed. My experience is that the actors will do well with this as long as they are given adequate support. Also, this is a good activity for your most socially capable actors to work with one another. They can collaborate to come up with meaningful portrayals of the characters in the scene.

It has been a challenge to find short scenes that are appropriate for the groups. The search for scenes with humor, scenes that are thought provoking, and scenes that touch on some of the issues with which our youngsters with AS are faced, have been difficult to find in published anthologies. However, sometimes reading scenes from these collections will spark an idea for a scene based on that general subject. You or another adult may want to write a scene based on that idea, but more relevant to your group. Writing scenes seemed daunting at first, but it really has not been so difficult. Also, perhaps another leader, a parent, or a local educator can help with finding and scripting scenes. In Appendix C there are a number of scenes that Susan March and I have written or adapted for the specific use of these groups. They are reproducible for use with your own groups.

Once you have assigned partners and scenes, send the groups off to highlight their lines and read through the script. The adults should circulate among the groups and discuss the meaning of the lines, the humor in the scene, and the characterizations. Once the actors are reasonably comfortable with reading the lines, the adult may want to suggest some simple movement, or "blocking." This could simply be that one actor is sitting at a table as the other enters, or that one character stands or moves on a given line.

Key skills

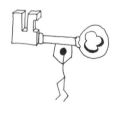

✓ Body awareness
✓ Working with others
✓ Using "Big 3"
✓ Reading "Big 3"
✓ Interpreting language

Next, call the actors back to "audience position" in preparation for the partners to perform their scenes for the group. It is a good idea to take a moment to review with the group what it means to be a good audience. Remind the actors to pick out some positive use of "The Big 3" by the actors in each scene. Audience members will be asked to share these observations after each scene. Also, after each scene, the director should debrief with the audience with the help of the actors who have just performed. Discuss the humor, the drama, and the social implications of the scene. An adult will have already done this debriefing with the actors while "directing" the scene. Encourage the actors to take the lead in the discussion about their scene. The actors will continue to work on these scenes during the remaining weeks. The scripts should go home in the actors' theater folders. Encourage them to try to memorize the lines if possible, but reassure them that they will be able to use their scripts as needed.

For younger groups, scenes should be about issues within your actors' experience. There is no need to tackle larger social issues within these scripts. With this age group you are working on basic emotion and line delivery. "Loose Tooth" has three six-year-olds talking about losing those baby teeth. In "A Ghostly Tale," one youngster tries to scare another with tales of ghosts. In "Playdate," friends do some simple problem solving. "Oh, Brother" explores the idea that being mean to your brother can have unwanted consequences. Most of these scenes also have an element of humor as well.

For the adolescent groups, however, there are many issues that can be addressed in partner scenes. "The Conversation," written by my colleague Susan March, addresses the issue of talking on and on about one's own interest without concern for the listener. It is a good script to use with one competent reader and two lesser readers, as the listeners in the scene have few lines, but many reactions. The script also deals with the subject with some humor. "Plane Talk" has a similar message, with a more dramatic subject matter. "Lesson from the Coach" brings up the issues of perfectionism and self-esteem. "The Day of the Jacket" is a funny scene that raises questions about truth vs. hurting someone's feelings vs. sending the wrong message. "Kool Kat" and "The Bully" both deal with peer issues, while "Sam's Strike Out" deals with parent–child issues. "Enough Already!" looks at a teen's frustration with his "perfect" sibling. These scenes give the actors a nice opportunity both for discussion, and for portraying a range of emotions.

Larger group scenes

Having the youngsters work in a larger group to put on a scene or skit is a great way to pull the group together to form a true "company" of actors. For the younger casts, traditional children's stories such as "The House that Jack Built" (see Box 5.2), "Green Eggs and Ham," "The Little Old Woman Who Swallowed a Fly" and "The Gingerbread Man" have worked well. Other recommended books and stories include "If You Give a Moose a Muffin" and other books in the Laura Geringer series. Using these types of stories works well because the actors do not necessarily need to have a lot of lines. An adult can narrate while the actors perform. Sometimes you will have an advanced reader who can handle the narration as well.

"The House that Jack Built" is a story that was recently staged with a very young group. This popular story has been published in many forms. It is a cumulative and repetitive story, making it perfect for our purposes. See Box 5.2 for how it could be narrated and performed. In this particular script the actors end up in a line across the front of the stage. *Hint*: it would be a good idea to assign roles and then line up the actors on the stage in the correct order before you even start working with the narration.

Key skills

✓ Sequencing
✓ Listening for cues
✓ Following directions
✓ Working in a group

Using hats, costumes and/or props can make these scenes a great deal of fun for the actors. You can go to the local goodwill store and scoop up lots of gems from the 50-cent tables. Brown, tan, or white shirts go a long way in creating animals when a creature hat is added to the mix. The girls love to put on dresses, even if they are too big! Sports coats and tacky ties are a great deal of fun! If you have time, for example, if you are running a weeklong camp, making hats and costumes can be fun as well. (See Chapter 8 on camp programs.)

The young actors will have a great many things to remember while doing these scenes. They will need to know the sequence of the action, when to put on costumes, where to go, what to do. It usually works best to teach the basics of the scene before you add the props and costumes, as these tend to add a distraction factor!

For the teenage groups, using "punchline scripts" has been very successful. Basically, these are jokes involving a number of characters, acted out in the form of a skit. See Box 5.3 for an example. Others are included in Appendix D of the book.

First you need to be sure everyone understands the joke in "Order in the Court." Then the actors can have a great deal of fun with this simple little skit. First, you have fun costumes for the characters: two policemen (hats and blue shirts), a judge (graduation gown works well), reporters and bailiff (goodwill sports coats and fedora hats for the reporters if you can find them), and Pebbles (a goodwill dress and a spray bottle of water!). Spend time having the actors consider what they want the audience to think during the scene, and how then to portray it. Of the characters in the skit, who knows that Pebbles is actually a person, and who does not? When do they first realize it and how do they react? When will the *audience* first realize it and how do you think they will react? Part of the social deficit for our youngsters with AS is their assumption that everyone thinks and knows what they do. This is a great opportunity to work on thinking about what other people are expected to know, and how they know it. It is imperative in acting as well as in real life to be able to make "smart guesses" about what people think and know (Winner 2002, p.24).

In more advanced groups comprising teens who have been in several previous classes, you may want to try a short one-act play that has multiple characters.

Box 5.2 Sample narration (bold) and actor's actions

The House that Jack Built

This is the house that Jack built. [*Jack smiles and points to the house.*]

This is the malt that lay in the house that Jack built. [*Jack places bag of "malt" on far right side of stage.*]

This is the rat that ate the malt that lay in the house that Jack built. [*Rat crawls across the stage and pretends to gobble malt.*]

This is the cat that killed the rat... [*Cat hurries across the stage and pretends to karate chop rat across back. Rat collapses.*]

...that ate the malt... [*Rat jumps up and eats malt.*]

...that lay in the house that Jack built. [*Jack smiles and points to the house.*]

This is the dog that worried the cat... [*Dog hurries across stage and chases cat in a small circle, barking.*]

...that killed the rat... [*Cat, back in original place next to rat, repeats karate chop. Rat collapses.*]

...that ate the malt... [*Rat jumps up, eats malt.*]

...that lay in the house that Jack built. [*Jack smiles and points to the house.*]

This is the cow with a crumpled horn, who tossed the dog... [*Cow enters, pretends to head-butt the dog (who is on all fours) in the side. Dog donkey-kicks legs up in back.*]

...that worried the cat... [*Dog chases cat, barks.*]

...that killed the rat... [*Karate chop, splat.*]

...that ate the malt... [*Slurp.*]

...that lay in the house that Jack built. [*Smile, point.*]

This is the maiden all forlorn who milked the cow with a crumpled horn... [*Sad maiden enters, pretends to milk the cow.*]

...who tossed the dog... [*Head-butt, donkey-kick.*]

...that worried the cat... [*Chase, bark.*]

...that killed the rat... [*HI-YAA! Splat!*]

...that ate the malt... [*Slurp.*]

...that lay in the house that Jack built. [*Smile, point.*]

This is the man all tattered and torn, who kissed the maiden all forlorn... [*Scruffy man enters, pretends to kiss maiden's hand.*]

...who milked the cow with the crumpled horn... [*Milk.*]

...who tossed the dog... [*Head-butt, donkey-kick.*]

...that worried the cat... [*Chase, bark.*]

...that killed the rat... [*HI-YAA! Splat!*]

...that ate the malt... [*Slurp.*]

...that lay in the house that Jack built. [*Forced smile, point.*]

This is the priest all shaven and shorn who married the man all tattered and torn... [*Priest enters, pretends to shave, opens book to marry man and maiden.*]

...who kissed the maiden all forlorn... [*Kiss hand.*]

...who milked the cow... [*Milk.*]

...who tossed the dog... [*Head-butt, donkey-kick.*]

...that worried the cat... [*Chase, bark.*]

...that killed the rat... [*HI-YAA! Splat!*]

...that ate the malt... [*Slurp.*]

...that lay in the house that Jack built. [*Jack is bored, points.*]

This is the cock that crowed in the morn... [*Cock enters, "Cock-a-doodle-doo."*]

...that woke the priest all shaven and shorn... [*Priest does big stretch and yawns.*]

...who married the man all tattered and torn... [*Priest opens book to marry.*]

...who kissed the maiden all forlorn... [*Kiss hand.*]

...who milked the cow... [*Milk.*]

...who tossed the dog... [*Head-butt, donkey-kick.*]

...that worried the cat... [*Chase, bark.*]

...that killed the rat... [*HI-YAA! Splat!*]

...that ate the malt... [*Slurp.*]

...that lay in the house that Jack built. [*Very bored, points lazily.*]

This is the farmer who sowed the corn... [*Farmer enters pretending to scatter seed saying "Here, chick, chick."*]

...who fed the cock that crowed in the morn... [*"Cock-a-doodle-doo".*]

...that woke the priest all shaven and shorn... [*Priest does big stretch and yawns.*]

...who married the man all tattered and torn... [*Priest opens book to marry.*]

...who kissed the maiden all forlorn... [*Kiss hand.*]

...who milked the cow... [*Milk.*]

...who tossed the dog... [*Head-butt, donkey-kick.*]

...that worried the cat... [*Chase, bark.*]

...that killed the rat... [*HI-YAA! Splat!*]

...that ate the malt... [*Slurp.*]

...that lay in the house that Jack built. [*Says, "Finally!" and points lazily.*]

[*Narrator leads cast to say this in unison.*]

And this is The House that Jack Built! [*All collapse on floor.*]

Box 5.3 Order in the Court

Order in the Court

Scene	*Courtroom. Judge is behind desk. Two policemen escort man into the courtroom. Judge pounds gavel three times.*
Bailiff:	Will the court please come to order? First case please!!
Judge:	What is this man accused of?
Policeman 1:	He was throwing pebbles in the lake!
Policeman 2:	And it isn't the first time either!
Man 1:	Your honor, they've got the wrong guy!
Judge:	Quiet! That's disgraceful! Give this man 30 days in jail! [*Policemen exit with prisoner 1*]
Reporter 1:	Breaking news! The judge gave the man 30 days just for throwing pebbles!?!

Reporter 2:	Stay tuned for further developments.
Judge:	Quiet in the courtroom!
Bailiff:	Yes, quiet in the courtroom! Next case please!!
Policeman 1:	Got another one your honor! [*Escorts another man into court.*]
Policeman 2:	Yep—throwing pebbles into the lake!
Man 2:	I'm innocent, I tell ya! I been framed!
Judge:	QUIET, YOU!!! Your behavior is disgraceful! Give this man 30 days in jail! [*Pounds gavel one time.*]
Reporter 1:	I really can't believe this, folks! I have never seen such a thing!
Reporter 2:	Me neither—30 days for throwing pebbles!! Unbelievable! Back to you, Tom.
Judge:	Order! Order! Quiet in the courtroom!
Girl:	Hello, your honor. I've just come from the lake. My name is Pebbles. [*Soaking wet.*]

Key skills

✓ Understanding the language of humor
✓ Executive function:
   ○ Sequencing
   ○ Organizing props and costumes
✓ Working with larger group

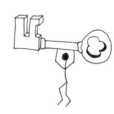

Chapter 6

Whose Line is it Anyhow?

Mary

Mary came into the first class with her head hanging low, avoiding eye contact. She remained on the periphery while the other actors arrived. It was fairly clear that her level of social impairment was significant. We were eventually able to get Mary engaged. Although I usually choose the partners for the paired activities, she requested a particular partner for the first activity. I honored her request, but then assigned her a partner for the next activity. Mary stomped over to her partner and Miss Susan, clearly unhappy.

She said in a loud voice, "I don't want to work with him. He's autistic!" Fortunately Doug did not seem to hear. Miss Susan took Mary aside and discussed the comment. She asked Mary how she thought Doug would feel if he had heard her comment and her tone. How would she feel if someone said something about not wanting to work with her? Mary sulked a few moments, then went over to work with Doug on their open scene. Miss Susan coached them, and by the time the group reconvened ten minutes later, they walked in with Mary offering Paula high five saying, "We were awesome, weren't we Paul?" With a big grin Paul returned the high five and said "Definitely!" And they were.

Improvisational games are a great way to work on skills such as shifting, reading cues, perspective taking. The following are examples of some games and activities, and how they address particular social skills.

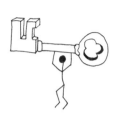

Key skills

✓ Taking a risk
✓ Thinking about what others know or may think
✓ Flexible thinking
✓ Knowing names of peers
✓ Waiting

Props

If you have seen the props game on the television show *Whose Line is it Anyway?*, you will have seen that they play with huge, oversized props that you would only see in a television or movie studio. Teams of two actors take turns using the prop as a specific object. In the television game actors can verbalize and make sounds. In the Acting Antics version of the game, start with one actor at a time, and use everyday objects. Consider using a large scarf, a colander, a ruler, a tray, a shoelace, a tennis racket. Equally challenging are any number of odd kitchen gadgets you may find in your drawer. Put out two objects at a time, so the actors can choose the one they prefer. The mission of the actor is to choose one of the objects and use it as something other than what it actually is. They must do this *without talking or making sounds*. The audience members will raise a hand when they think they know what the object is, or what the actor is doing. An audience member must wait to be called on by the performer before he or she verbalizes a guess. The performer should be encouraged to call on audience members by name.

Again, the challenge for the actors is to recognize what the audience knows or doesn't know about what the actor is thinking. For example, perhaps an actor chooses to use the large scarf as a beach blanket. The actor unfolds the scarf and lays it on the ground, spreading it out with care. She sits and then lies down on the scarf. An audience member guesses that it is a bed. The difficulty lies in the fact that the actor *knows* that she is using the scarf as a beach blanket, but the audience cannot know that unless she gives them more information. This is a difficult concept for individuals with AS because their wiring often makes them assume that others think and know what they think and know. So now, if our actor pantomimes putting on sunscreen and sunglasses, our audience will be able to understand that it is a beach blanket in this scenario.

Another example of this is that the actor might choose to pantomime a very obscure and specific character from a comic book or video game. This is done without recognition that all or most of the audience will have no frame of reference for this and will not be able to make a reasonable guess. Again, it is important to work on helping the actors think about what the audience is likely to know.

The actors really enjoy the props game, but often some guidelines need to be established. Many of the actors want to pantomime that the object is some sort of weapon. Once one actor does this, it is often repeated in many different forms. Establishing a "no weapons" rule from the beginning is a good idea. Falling into a 1960s "flower child" pose and showing them the peace sign, you can tell them you made the rule because you believe in "peace, love and brotherhood, man." The actors will probably roll their eyes and protest mildly, and then move on. The other main reason for dissuading them from the fighting or weaponry pantomime is because it is just too easy for them to fall into that repeatedly. Challenge them to be more creative. As the director, you will need to decide what parameters you want to set up, both creatively and philosophically.

"Taxi Driver"

This is a game that will be in top demand once you introduce it to the actors! It can get a bit frantic, so you want to be sure to set up the structure to contain the craziness. Arrange four chairs to simulate a car—two in front, two in back. The actors will be rotating in and out of the car at a rapid pace, so you will want to teach them the rotation pattern first. Have three actors sit in three of the seats, leaving the driver's seat empty. The new person to the car will always enter via the driver's seat. Have an adult or actor sit in the driver's seat. Now the car is full. Next a new person will approach the car to enter. The actors in the car rotate as follows (see Figure 6.1):

1.   The passenger in the back left gets out of the car and goes back in line.

2.   The passenger back right moves to back left.

3.   Front right moves to back right.

4.   Driver moves to front right.

5.   New driver enters.

Practice the rotation before even explaining the rest of the game. It has worked for me to get them set in their positions, and then just clap my hands and say, "Switch." I just keep repeating it until everyone has rotated through. Then the actors are back in the original position, and the game can be explained.

In this game, the driver coming into the taxi is in control. That actor assumes a character or persona, and the rest of the actors in the cab follow suit, imitating the driver's character. For example, an actor comes into the driver seat and starts talking

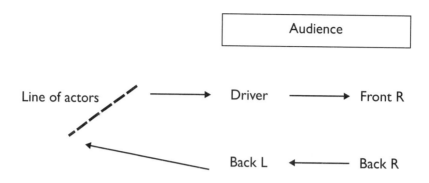

Figure 6.1 Diagram for rotation in "Taxi Driver"

and moving like a robot. All the actors in the car should then act and talk like robots. This will only go on for 15 to 20 seconds before the director claps and says, "Switch." Then everyone rotates, and the next actor comes into the driver seat all bent over and talking in the hoarse voice of an elderly man. Perhaps he says, "Let's get down to the senior center." The others begin talking like old folks as well, maybe saying something like, "All right. I've got my new dentures so I'm ready!" Another might say, "Did anybody bring extra Depends?", and so on. In "Taxi Driver" the rule is that, if you don't know what character the actor is doing then fake it! Just try to imitate what he is doing or how he is talking or acting the best you can. Remind the actors that it moves very quickly, so if they are stumped, the character will change very soon.

Key skills

✓ Motor planning
✓ Sequencing
✓ Shifting
✓ Response time

As mentioned earlier, this game can get pretty frantic, but is a great deal of fun. However, some of your actors may have a very difficult time coming up with a character. Before playing the game, you may want to brainstorm character ideas as a group and write them on a poster or whiteboard. This is also a good time to dissuade some of your actors from choosing to do very specific characters from movies or video games, because it is likely that the others will have no idea what they are doing. The list should comprise mostly general character types that are easily understood and imitable (see Box 6.1 for a list of potential characters for this game). Please be sure to have your actors help you come up with your group's own list, but the list in Figure 6.2 can give you some ideas where to start.

This game is a good workout for your actors for many reasons. One of the difficulties in AS mentioned earlier is that ability to "shift". This game is all about shifting very quickly from one character to another by following the lead of another person. It is more difficult for some of the actors than others, but in this fun format everyone can be successful. Be sure to know who may need some cueing and do so with little fanfare, so that no actor experiences undue anxiety.

Box 6.1 Potential characters for "Taxi Driver"

bratty child	gangster	robot
space alien	witch	race car driver
snob	Mr. S-L-O-W talker	"American Idol" guy
nervous guy/girl	back seat driver	cowboy/girl
Barney	hyper guy/girl	Mr. Know-it-all

"Scenes from a hat"

This game is adapted from one of the games on *Whose Line…* on television. In the Acting Antics version, individual cards are placed in a hat. On each card is written a simple conflict situation that might typically occur in the age group of your actors. An example would be as follows: "One brother is caught red handed by the other brother in his room playing with his video game system. What happens?" The trick is that they have to resolve the situation in some way during a very short

Key skills

✓ Reading the nonverbal signals of others
✓ Responding to the signals of others
✓ Problem solving
✓ Recognizing the perspective of others

conversation. Often adults and/or NT actors might model this first. The focus is on reading the other person and reacting accordingly. If John comes in screaming, Pete might react a certain way. If Pete is apologetic, John might react differently.

In a group setting, the role of the audience in this activity is very important. The actors watching the performers will need to analyze what happened, who reacted first, how did the second person react to the first, and how did it end. How could John and Pete have had a different outcome? In some cases you may want to have the same actors do the scene again after the discussion. Or you might have two other actors provide different reactions, causing a different outcome. For some actors this will definitely be a challenge. You may find you need to "kick start" them by feeding an initial line. Again, it is important to challenge the actor without causing a great deal of anxiety, so it will be important for the adults to be observant and sensitive.

"Blah, Blah"

"Blah, Blah" is an activity I use with more advanced groups, once they have "The Big 3" fairly well mastered. It is actually somewhat of a variation on "Scenes from a Hat", but with a new twist. This time, when the actors perform a scenario, they may not use actual words. Instead they will only say, "Blah, Blah." They must show the meaning of the words by using "The Big 3": vocal tone, body language and facial expressions. For example, let us imagine that the scenario is a teenager who has come home late and mom is waiting. Mom might say, "And *where* have you *been*?" in a tone that is clearly angry.

Key skills
✓ Understanding meaning with *only* nonverbal cues
✓ Reacting to another in response to his or her nonverbal communication
✓ Ending a conversation

The actor should now say, "Blah, *blah*, blah, blah, *blah*?" instead of the actual words, perhaps crossing her arms and posing in an angry stance. It would also be important that the voice goes up at the end to indicate the inflection of a question. Now the actor playing the teen must decide whether she is going to be apologetic, rebellious, dismissive, or silent, and indicate that response through her tone, face and body language, while saying only, "blah, blah." For example, let's say the actor playing the teen decides to answer with a flip "Whatever." Instead of those actual words she would say "Blah blah blah" in the same tone she would have used had she said "Whatever." If she rolls her eyes and tosses her hair over her shoulder as she says it, the meaning should be pretty clear. Then the actor playing the parent should respond appropriately. Again the goal is to bring the scene to an end. This particular scenario has been ended in a variety of ways in my experience. In one group the teen was grounded and sent to her room; in another the mom and teen hugged and all was forgiven. In yet another portrayal the teen stomped off to her room; in another the mom went to *her* room in tears. All these scenes were portrayed only using "blah, blah."

An important component to this activity is once again the analysis by the actors in the audience. This is partly why it is more effective with the more advanced groups. It is so interesting to hear them "interpret" the scene. They have actually made statements like, "She sassed her mom and then the mom grounded her, and she stomped off to her room." When asked, "What do you mean? All I heard was blah, blah, blah," they told me exactly what the various inflections, postures and expressions used by the actors meant. Hopefully this is an activity that clearly illustrates how much we communicate *without* words.

"Freeze"

This is a challenging game and one rarely used with younger groups of actors. Like "Taxi Driver" it requires the actor to process on the spot. However, in "Taxi Driver" the actors entering the car can come up with any character they want, irrespective of what has gone on in the car before they entered. On the contrary, in "Freeze" the actor needs to make a response based on what the actors are doing before he enters the scene.

Key skills

✓ Improving processing speed
✓ Imitation of physical position
✓ Shifting the topic based on physical position
✓ Initiating conversation

Two actors begin on stage by having a conversation based on a cue from the director. For example, the director has said, "You are two friends talking about a video game."

The subject in this game is really insignificant; it is the physicality of the scene that is most important. Two actors (actor A and actor B) begin the scene, incorporating as many large gestures and different body positions as possible. The director shouts, "Freeze," hopefully while the actors are in interesting poses. The actors (A and B) freeze were they are. A waiting actor (C) now comes in, taps the shoulder of either one of the posed actors (A or B). The actor who was tapped exits (let's say it was actor B), and the incoming actor (C) assumes the posed position of his predecessor (B). Now the new actor (C) must begin a new scene with actor A based only on their physical positions.

Hopefully, a specific example will help to clarify this. *Scene 1*: Amy (A) says to Fred (B), "This is my dog, Oscar." Fred bends down to pet the imaginary dog. "Freeze!" *Scene 2*: Joe (C) comes in and taps Fred. Fred exits and Joe assumes the bent down position, but now says, "Hey, it's my lucky day…I just found a $10 dollar bill on the ground." Amy (A) says, "Hey that's mine. I must have dropped it." Joe (C) responds, "No way, man. I found it." Fred puts both hands on his head in frustration. "Freeze!" *Scene 3*: Now Paul (D) enters and taps Fred who exits. Paul puts his hands on his head and perhaps says to Joe, "Coach I told you this helmet was too small…I can't get it off!" A visual representation of each scene can be seen in Figure 6.3.

So the "shifting" occurs by an actor coming in and assuming the physical position of one of the other actors. The entering actor always initiates the new scene, which should have nothing in common with the previous scene, except the physical position of the entering actor. As you can imagine, this game presents many challenges for any actors, and presumably even more for our actors diagnosed with social cognition deficits.

The entering actor must:

- decide which actor they will replace

- emulate the position of that actor

- begin a new scene based on the physical position they have assumed

- be sure they are beginning a new scene and not just continuing the previous one.

The other actor needs to:

- freeze when told

- wait for the incoming actor to begin a dialogue

- observe and determine the context of the new scene as established by that actor

- shift and respond to this new character in an entirely new context.

Figure 6.2 Visual representation of scenes in "Freeze"

Before embarking on this game, you may want to do the following activity to help with the idea of body position and context. Have an adult or actor stand with his hands up in the air. What context could be invented for this position? Consider the following:

- He is being held up by a robber.

- He is trying to reach something up high.

- He is exercising.

- He is waving in an airplane on a runway.

Here's another. Have an actor bend down with her hands toward the floor. Consider the following:

- She is about to hike a football.

- She is about to pick up something.

- She is looking at evidence of a UFO on the ground.

- She just hurt her back and can't stand up.

- She is doing deep knee bends.

- She has lost her contact lens.

Key skills

✓ Motor planning/imitation
✓ Taking a risk
✓ Initiating
✓ Reacting
✓ Creative thinking

You get the idea. Emphasize the importance of using some big gestures and/or postures in this game, so it is easier to shift to a new context. Another word of advice—it is my personal policy to restrict the scene from having to do with fighting and chasing. When this restriction has not been in place, every second scene is about fighting and/or chasing. It is just too easy to go that way, and that the actors need to be more creative than that. Again consider establishing the ground rules from the beginning.

The actors do not necessarily form a line for this game. It is pretty much left for someone to enter when they have an idea. However, some will jump in each time without regard for the others who are waiting. This is a good opportunity for incidental teaching. Have a discussion about what other actors are thinking about someone who has taken five turns when others have had only one. There may also be some actors who are either not brave enough to enter, or who need significant assistance. There is no harm in slowing the game down, assisting an actor in how to take position, and even giving some ideas about the context. For that actor, thinking up something to say within that context is challenge enough.

"Freeze" is a game geared more toward the larger group setting. However, the lead-up activities of thinking up new contexts for different physical positions could be readily practiced at home or in a smaller therapy setting.

"Slow News Day"

This is an activity in which the group (three or four actors) chooses a subject from a list of common items (see list in Appendix A). The task is to create a news story centered around that item. The group must work together to come up with the story, which can be as ridiculous as they would like it to be. Next they need to decide who will fill the various roles on the news team (see "Slow News Day" planning sheet in Appendix B). One person may be the anchor; others may do weather, sports, or traffic. Some groups have added a "man on the street" character.

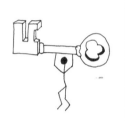

Key skills

✓ Group interaction
✓ Collaboration
✓ Compromise
✓ Creative thinking

This is a great collaborative activity, and groups are likely to need some facilitation in order to be sure that all opinions are respected and that compromise can be reached. The actors are generally very creative, so ideas are usually abundant!

This can also be a fun family activity with everyone taking the role of one of the news team. It can be a way for a classroom teacher to have students explore and report on real current events, or even on an academic concept. For example, "In today's breaking news, Ben Franklin has made an amazing discovery about electricity!" You could then have a news anchor, Susie Sparks, who narrates the story, sending it over to her colleagues when appropriate. The weather person, Theo Thunder, could speak about the necessary weather conditions for Ben Franklin's kite caper, and a man on the street could give perspective on how life was before electricity and how it will change. This can be done relaying the necessary facts, but also using humorous characters to bring the facts to life.

"Monkey in the Middle"

This improvisational game would be used for a teen group that has had some previous experience in your workshops, as it is quite challenging. The activity requires three people. One person is the "pivot person" who will stand between the other two actors. The actors on each sides are given a paper on which two phrases are written (see Box 6.2 for sample phrases). Those two phrases are the only phrases those actors may say during the scene. The "Flexible Phrases" activity described in Chapter 4 is a good warm-up for this activity, and actors should show competence in that activity before attempting "Monkey in the Middle."

The third actor, the pivot person in the middle, has free range of what he or she may say. The middle person is designated to be an employer or boss training two new employees. The audience is asked to suggest a type of business or workplace, and that suggestion sets the scene. As the scene begins, the boss (middle) welcomes the two trainees and begins to improvise dialogue about the training. It is now the job of the two side actors (the trainees) to insert their two phrases any time they can use them appropriately. The goal is to change the delivery ("Big 3") in order to alter the meaning of the phrase. Just like as "Flexible Phrases" (Chapter 4), the phrases can mean different things when the "Big 3" is changed, or when the context is changed.

In this game an adult should assume the middle position so that he or she can assure the actors' success. If the adult writes the phrases, he or she can then create dialogue that will make it easier for the trainee to insert his phrase. It is important to have the phrases written on a card, so that each actor can keep the card in hand as a visual reminder of the phrases. This way, the adult in the middle position can also refer to the card as needed. With an actor who is less proficient at this game, the adult can provide an obvious verbal cue and then allow some pause time, giving the actor the opportunity to say the phrase. If the actor does not respond after the verbal cue and some pause time, the adult can actually point to the appropriate phrase on the actor's card.

One of the reasons the teens like this game so much is that it is not only fun to play but also very entertaining to watch. As the frustration of the "boss" character grows, so does the audience's laughter. For this reason it is advisable to have an adult who really understands the game model the "boss" role a number of times. The adult should gradually build the frustration in his or her tone, gestures, and facial expression, adding to the comedic value of the scene. (Our actors in the audience would be rolling with laughter by the time the scene ended.) The adult can also set up cues for the "trainees" to help make it easier for them to insert their phrases. That middle adult can also steer the dialogue so that there is a natural ending to the scene.

Box 6.2 Sample phrases for "Monkey in the Middle"

	Phrase 1	**Phrase 2**
Trainee #1	That's no good.	Are you sure?
Trainee #2	I don't think so.	How does that work?

	Phrase 1	**Phrase 2**
Trainee #1	You're good at that.	What are you doing?
Trainee #2	I'm not ready.	Can you repeat that?

	Phrase 1	**Phrase 2**
Trainee #1	Hey, stop that.	What is that?
Trainee #2	You've got to be joking.	Can we go now?

Although we have primarily done this scene with a leader in the middle role, eventually there were a few actors in the group who wanted to portray the employer after watching numerous times.

In some cases the leader may not feel that the group can jump into this game successfully. In those cases one might begin by having the actors read the sample script (see Box 6.3) along with the interpretations. Then perhaps three actors or one adult and two actors could read the script as written, trying to portray the meaning as written in the sample. This is a good pre-teaching strategy and might give the actors a better idea of how to deliver the lines in a variety of ways. You may want to script a few scenes like this until the actors get more comfortable with the game. It could also be played with each "trainee" having only one phrase until the actors become more confident.

Skills in "Monkey in the Middle"

Besides reinforcing previously learned skills such as using and reading the "Big 3", this game introduces the more advanced actors to new challenges. They not only need to attend closely to the dialogue, but they also need to constantly be pondering if and how their phrases can be inserted. This requires a great deal of thinking on one's feet, including processing information fairly quickly and then responding appropriately with one of the phrases. In order to make the scenes funny, the youngsters need to grasp the concept of the game and the humor involved. This involves understanding that words and phrases can have multiple meanings.

Key skills

✓ Using "Big 3"
✓ Using multiple meanings of words and phrases
✓ Focusing
✓ Unrehearsed reacting to the delivery of others

Box 6.3 Example of "Monkey in the Middle" dialogue: two phrases improvisation

Setting: A pet store owner training two new employees

John's phrases: "I don't think so.", "Why are you doing that?"

Ed's phrases: "You're good at that.", "Can we go now?"

	What the character is saying	**What the character is thinking**
Owner:	Welcome to Pets R'Us. We are happy to have you here at our orientation.	
John:	Why are you doing that?	Why are you being so annoyingly perky?
Owner:	Why am I doing what? I'm just welcoming you.	What's your problem? I'm just trying to be nice.
Ed:	You're good at that.	You are good at being perky and obnoxious.
Owner:	Why, thank you. Now, every day you will report here at 8 a.m.	This guy is OK. Now let's get down to business.
John:	I don't think so.	I really don't know if I can get up that early.
Owner:	Well that's not a great attitude for your first day!	Yikes, this guy's going to be a problem.

Ed:	Can we go now?	Can we just go into the store and get working?
Owner:	I'm glad you're anxious to get started, but you have to know some of the basics first. Now, each morning you will need to clean out the animals' cages. [*Demonstrating.*]	
John:	I don't think so.	I can't stand the smell. I have a weak stomach!
Ed:	[*To Owner.*] You're good at that.	I'm going to get on this guy's good side!
Owner:	[*To John.*] You need to change your attitude son! [*To Ed.*] Of course I'm good at that, I've been doing it for ten years! [*To both.*] OK, put these gloves on and give it a try.	
John:	Why are you doing that? [*Holding his nose.*]	Why are you making me do this? I'm going to get sick.
Ed:	Can we go now? [*Pleading and gesturing to owner to move away from John.*]	Can we go somewhere far from this guy who's going to get sick any minute?
Owner:	Why exactly did you come here if you didn't expect to work!! Let's move on to something else.	
John:	I don't think so.	I don't think I can do this job!!
Owner:	[*To John.*] I can't believe some of the people the agency sends me! You are fired!	
John:	I DON'T THINK SO! [*He storms off.*]	You're not firing me. I QUIT!
Ed:	You're good at that!	
Owner:	Yeah, I am aren't I? Let's get to work.	I like this kid!

Chapter 7

Starting Your Own Troupe

Allen

I was asked to speak to a local education group about the Antics program. I decided it would be most effective to have my actors demonstrate some of the activities and scenes. Six of my teens were recruited, and we met one evening to decide what they would perform. I prepared the actors, outlining the structure of the evening for them. The evening would include a buffet dinner, some very brief introductions, and our presentation. The evening arrived, the actors ate their dinners, and suddenly the moderator announced that we were each to introduce ourselves to the group. You could visibly see the anxiety rise in the faces of my young actors. Allen was looking especially unnerved, as he was to be the first of our group to introduce himself. I held my breath for Allen as the introductions moved around the table toward him. When his turn arrived, Allen said, "My name is Allen, and I'm 16 and...well...that's about it." Once Allen had his turn, the others seemed to relax a bit, and each introduced themselves in turn. As we left the room to prepare for our presentation, Allen said to me with a huge sigh, "Well, THAT was unexpected!"

So now you've begun to use many of these activities, and you are ready to do more. You would like to get more adults and actors involved, but the task seems daunting. It's not nearly as tough as it sounds, and will be well worth all your efforts. To have a whole group of young actors find success, build self-esteem, have fun, and blossom in front of an audience is an indescribable feeling of accomplishment. So read on, and consider trying to organize some fellow parents or professionals to offer this wonderful growth opportunity to more youngsters in your area.

Finding a space

Finding a space in which to hold your program can be a challenge at first. Once your program is up and running, and families and professionals can see the success, offers for performance space should come your way. A local community theater may offer their facilities during off hours as a community service. You can present the program in conjunction with a local YMCA or a community recreation organization. One workshop was run and performed in a parent's home.

A local school district had heard about the positive outcomes of the program through some parents, and contracted me to run a program as an Extended School Year (ESY) option for secondary students diagnosed with AS. ESY services are IEP driven and provided when there is evidence that a student will regress in certain goal areas during an extended break from programming. The district provided a great environment where we worked in a real theater setting. We had students working with stage lighting and a curtain. Keep in mind that having a full stage, curtains, and lighting is far from the usual occurrence! The program can be run effectively in a variety of spaces. You basically need a room with little clutter and enough open space in which to move and perform.

Time factor

How you configure your workshops will depend largely on your own availability and time constraints. Groups during the school year typically run one night a week for four to six weeks. Each individual session is generally two hours. The start time works well at 6 p.m., as opposed to immediately after school, because people come a distance to get there. Additionally, several parents expressed that anything that ran past 8 p.m. was too late on a school night.

In the summer, on the other hand, the groups are run more like a camp program. Sessions occur daily, two to four hours each day, depending on the age and attention span of the group. The camp runs for one or even two weeks. Eventually the hope is to run four-week camps, especially for the teens. The summer groups provide more time to incorporate other skills such as basic scene design and backdrop painting. This will be discussed further in Chapter 8.

Help please!

Working with any group of youngsters, it is always a good idea to have at least two adults present at each session. First, for safety purposes that just makes sense. If someone were to get hurt or sick, or wander away from the group, you always want to have someone there to stay with the group while you attend to the youngster in need.

Additionally, it is great to have another adult who can circulate as you split the actors into smaller groups for activities. The groups will definitely need facilitation for them to be successful. Also, the adults can help model for the actors. There may also be specific times when you will want to pair a student who is having some difficulty with an adult rather than a peer.

Several professionals have volunteered to assist in the Acting Antics workshops and that has been wonderful. It is very beneficial to design and plan these workshops with a partner, someone with whom you work extremely well. I am really fortunate now to be working with a colleague, Susan March, who is an Autism Consultant and Occupational Therapist. To have the opportunity to plan, collaborate and then debrief with someone is a wonderful asset. It also is helpful because sometimes actors will react differently to each adult personality. Finding a kindred soul who really wants to go on this adventure with you makes it a terrific ride!

Additionally, don't hesitate to use volunteers in your groups. More hands and models are always useful. Besides, having volunteers is a great way to get others to learn what you are doing and eventually branch out to create their own programs.

Getting the word out

There is a variety of ways to let the community know about your drama group. Contact your local support groups, parent groups, and schools. People are always looking for ways to teach these youngsters social understanding, so your target group is definitely out there. Once you have run a few sessions and the word gets out, you may well have a waiting list! Groups of six to ten actors are recommended for the younger students (ages 8 to 13). Groups of eight to twelve actors would be appropriate for the older students (ages 14 up). You may also get inquiries from parents of youngsters diagnosed with nonverbal learning disorders or other diagnoses involving social cognition deficits. This approach would certainly be appropriate for those individuals.

Neurotypical actors

If at all possible it is great to add some NT peers to your groups. In my case, my affiliation with the community theater gave me a wonderful pool of youngsters. Because of their experiences performing for the camp program, and our diversity discussions, it was very easy for me to find volunteers willing and able to participate in our groups. However, my actors were now mostly teens so I needed to look elsewhere for peers for the younger group. Networking with elementary schoolteacher friends was all I needed to do to find some enthusiastic volunteers.

The NT peers need to have a basic understanding of AS so that they know why some of the unexpected behaviors or comments occur. It is important, though, that the NT actors participate along with the actors as *peers*, and not as staff. At the same time, they can model an activity, or pair up with a student with a more severe social impairment who might have difficulty if paired with another AS student for an activity. Try to have two to four NT peers in each group, but that definitely varies according to availability.

Actor background information

As the actors arrive for the first session, give the parents an introductory letter with your contact information, the date and time for your final showcase (see Figure 7.1 sample letter). Additionally, the parents or caregivers should fill out a short information form about their actor. Demographic information and emergency contact numbers should be included. Other information should include allergy and medical information, and also the parents' view on what they perceive to be their youngster's "top three" social issues. A question you may want to ask is whether or not the youngster is aware of their diagnosis. Although this is not directly addressed in class, discussions between actors, especially in the teen groups, do occur. Be sure to ask for photo/video permission. Video can be a great teaching tool, and it's nice for the actors to have photos as memorabilia when possible. A reproducible sample intake/registration form is provided (see Appendix B).

During the arrival time you will be meeting parents and their aspiring actors. Begin the group with adults wearing nametags, and have nametags ready for the actors. Occasionally a parent will arrive with a reluctant participant in tow. Sometimes it helps to give that youngster a job such as handing out the nametags. During this somewhat chaotic arrival time, you will get a quick glimpse of the youngsters in your group before the structured activities begin. You will see how each student reacts to a novel and unstructured time with unfamiliar people. One may pace, another may find a remote corner of the room. Occasionally you will

Acting Antics
THEATRE CLASS

Dear Parents,

We are looking forward to a great session of Acting Antics theatre classes! We will be doing theatre games, skits and scenes, and making friends! The actors will receive folders today, and they will need to bring them to and from class each week. Please check the folder for any notes or updates. The actors will also have some basic scripts and other papers they should keep in the folder.

We will culminate the week with a final performance the final Wednesday evening. Actors will come at 6:00 as usual, and our showcase will begin at 7:15. Please plan to attend and bring family and friends! If you have any questions, please see me before or after camp any day. I can also be reached at xxx@xxx.net or at my home phone # xxx-xxx-xxxx. If you would need to reach me during camp hours, call my cell phone: xxx-xxx-xxxx. (I would appreciate it if that # was only used for emergencies.)

Thanks so much for your support. Thanks for sharing your youngsters with me for a few weeks!

Cindy Schneider
Acting Antics

Figure 7.1 Sample letter

have the youngster who introduces themselves to each person. There have been those who explore every corner of the room and touch every visible item. There have been "scowlers," who look like they would rather be tortured than be there! Take a moment to observe the actors during this initial period, so that you can appreciate the growth you will see by the end of your session.

Parents who are bringing their youngsters for the first time often ask if they should stay around during the first class. After finding out what the particular concerns are, you can make that decision together with the parent. In general, the actors tend to participate more fully when the parents are not in the room, but I have certainly made exceptions. Additionally, some parents have waited in a nearby room, in the car, or just poked their head in a few times during the session. Just be sure you have the cell phone/emergency number for each parent, just in case.

Chapter 8

Ready Or Not, Here They Come!

Brad

We were having a week-long camp program for teens. Brad attended with a therapeutic support assistant to help him with his behavior and coping skills. On the first day of a new group the schedule is often somewhat less than exact, because it is difficult to know the attention span of the group. That first day Brad was very disruptive. He constantly interrupted, questioned, criticized, and so on. His assistant was having no success in keeping him engaged and appropriate. Finally I escorted Brad from the room, and listed very explicitly the expectation for the group. When we returned he was somewhat more successful. I went home that evening and began to design a behavior system that would address Brad's needs, and create a more positive experience for him. I tightened up the schedule, adding more detail. Upon arrival the next morning, Brad went and read the schedule, joined the group and participated without difficulty! I never even needed to use the behavior system. It appeared that it was the newness of the experience that caused him difficulty. Once he knew the routine, he relaxed and enjoyed himself.

Creating structure

So now you have your space and your group and are ready to begin. Before the group arrives, designate areas in the room to be your stage area, an audience area, and an area for the actors to put their personal belongings, scripts, etc. If this is established at the first session, it will make it easier to have the students fall into a routine.

Creating a schedule is also very important for many of the actors (see Figure 8.1 for a sample schedule). As in so many other situations, a great deal of anxiety can be eliminated if the youngsters are given predictability.

Generally, putting specific times on the schedule is not recommended because you want to have a little flexibility. If your schedule says that warm-ups go on until 10:20, then you had better not stop at 10:19 or at 10:21! There are bound to be some actors who will hold you to it. A sequence of activities provides predictability with flexibility. For teen groups you may want to print an individual agenda for the actors; for the younger groups, post the schedule.

Group dynamics

Every group of people, whether a club, organization, or team of teachers, has its own set of dynamics. Now consider the range of abilities, deficits, and personalities inherent in the diagnosis of AS. That range brings particular dynamics to the theater groups. Some of the actors who display more obvious social deficits are intolerant of others who also show significant deficits. Some of the youngsters who are somewhat more aware socially are not particularly tolerant of those who have more obvious social deficits. I have seen this dynamic in many different situations. I suspect that as these youngsters become more aware of their own deficits, they do not want to be grouped together with those more obviously impaired. It becomes a delicate balance to work on acceptance while also recognizing the reasons for the sensitivity. Pairing the more socially able actors together initially sometimes helps to build their own confidence. Later in the sessions, the same actors have often worked with anyone in the group without difficulty.

There are times when there is a real personality conflict, or a negative past experience between particular youngsters that makes partnering tough. One pair of boys in one of my teen summer camps attended middle school together. They clearly had developed a negative relationship. One was a "nudge" while the other had no tolerance. Our nudge needed to understand how others perceived his behavior. Our "intolerant one" needed to learn how to "filter" his comments. These issues became a primary focus in our group, because if not addressed they were going to be very disruptive.

In another teen group it became clear that one young lady had a bit of a crush on a young man. He, however, did not have a mutual feeling toward this young lady. She was passing him notes and getting upset because he would not respond. We had an opportunity in this smaller group to work on these issues and coach both parties in better ways to approach or respond to the other.

Day 1 Schedule

Sample day 1 schedule for an adolescent group that meets for 2 hours, once a week, for 5–6 weeks.

6:00 Ice Breaker—Introduce "The Big 3"

- Review set-up of room
- Review schedule of activities

6:15 Circle Activities

- Actors introduce themselves
- Name game
- Who has the Power?
- Bamboozle

6:45 Actor's Rules

- Review rules and encourage discussion
- See if anyone wants to make a poster

7:00 Flexible Phrases

- Assign partners
- Give one or two phrases to each pair
- Actors work in pairs for five minutes
- Regroup to audience position—each pair performs phrases

7:20 Silly Skit

- Introduce skit
- Assign roles—perform
- Switch roles—perform
- Discuss humor in skit from audience perspective

7:40 Taxi Driver

- Brainstorm and write list of possible characters
- Practice rotation scheme
- Model a round with helpers, more cognizant actors
- Play a round if time allows

7:55 Regroup in circle

- Announcements

Figure 8.1 Sample schedule

So besides the structured acting activities in which we are targeting specific skills, the dynamics of working in a large group toward a common goal is an ongoing objective throughout the sessions. Many "teachable moments" occur and should be utilized. This is the application of the skills that we really want them to learn.

"Sell Your Partner"

One specific activity that can be a great way for your teen actors to get to know each other is through an activity called "Sell Your Partner." This is an improvisation activity for your older groups that involves some preparation, but is not entirely scripted. Partners are assigned and each actor is given a graphic organizer on which to gather information (see sample form in Appendix B). The partners interview one another in order to get information about the partner's skills, interests, family, etc. Notes can be made on the organizer so that actors can use that sheet as a visual tool during the activity. Once the information is gathered, each actor practices doing a "sales pitch" in order to "sell" his or her partner to the audience.

In preparation for this activity we talk about the caricature of the "used car salesman." One of my more advanced or NT actors might demonstrate the technique by selling us the shoes they are wearing. We will make note of the vocal tone, body language, and the persuasive language used in order to convince the audience that they need this "product".

The actors have great fun with this. Some have created a business name for themselves. An example of this would be, "Come on down to J.R. Smith's on the corner of Main and Spruce!" Some have added incentives and disclaimers as well. One youngster said, "Buy one today and you will get a free toaster!" He then added in a fast, quieter voice, "Toasters not available Monday through Friday or on the weekend."

Key skills

✓ Peer interaction
✓ Use of "Big 3"
✓ Speaking extemporaneously using a cue card
✓ Learning to appreciate others' strengths
✓ Self-esteem through hearing own strengths "advertised"

This activity facilitates the actors in getting to know their peers, and yet provides a framework via the graphic organizer that makes the interview process easy for them. The actor then needs to share the interests and skills of their partner with the audience in a fun and dramatic manner. Some of the scripts that the actors have created have included the following statements:

- If you need someone to help you with your homework, Ruth is the one for you! She is good at every subject!

- Do you need someone to help you get to the next level in that video game? Call on Karl!!

- Need somebody to walk your dog? Paul's the guy for you because he *loves* animals!

Truthfully, I expected this to be harder for these actors than it was. They did extremely well with it, and their pitches were hilarious! Each brought a great deal of originality to the activity, and when they performed it more than once it was different each time!

Chapter 9

Antics Summer Camp

Pete

Pete was a tall, good-looking high school student who had just completed a very difficult school year. He had been treated recently for severe depression. Pete came into the first day of our acting camp with his head hanging low. He mumbled during the introductions and looked only at the floor. He quietly told me he wasn't sure he wanted to perform. I told him to watch a while and see what he thought. He sat out a few games and then quietly joined in. His voice was still very soft and his gaze down. The second day during one activity, he began to use a British accent. He was so good at it! The other actors praised him and laughed at his comedy. His head raised slightly and his voice became ever so slightly louder. By the end of the week, Pete's talent was very evident. Not only was he a master of accents and characters, but a graphic artist as well. His group relied on him to do the detail work on their backdrop. By the end of the week his head was held high and he was fully engaged with the activities and with his fellow actors!

Time frame

Having week-long camp sessions in the summer is a great way to run the acting program. Having three-hour sessions daily for an entire week or more has many advantages. The actors get to know each other more quickly and develop a better rapport. There is more time to work on scenes and activities. There is more carryover from class to class since the days are consecutive. This format allows time for a snack and social break, and for work on scenery.

Snack and social break

This has emerged as an important time during our summer sessions. It allows the actors some downtime in which they can share interests, get to know one another and/or just decompress from the demands of the group. It gives the leaders an opportunity to observe the actors in unstructured time to better recognize their social strengths and deficits. For the younger groups, significant facilitation may be needed to have the actors engage with one another. In one group we had been working on the "joke scripts" and one of the youngsters brought in a joke book. Break times were then spent with the actors sharing jokes with one another. The facilitation was needed to assist them in allowing everyone a turn, and being polite listeners, etc.

Key skills

✓ Informal socializing
✓ Having conversations with peers
✓ Finding common interests

For the teen groups, less facilitation is needed for many of the actors. They seem to find a niche after the first day. As they cluster into groups, conversations about video game progress, cartooning techniques, and movies are heard. However, there always seem to be two or three actors who either gravitate only to the adults, or stay alone on the periphery. The NT actors can be of significant assistance here. Once the leader has observed and gotten a feel for the group, he or she can prompt the NT actors to invite the lone actor to join their group. This is usually effective. This is also where the "special interests" information, written by the parents on the intake form, can be of great use. The NT can be coached to start an interaction about that student's interest and attempt to draw others into the conversation.

Scenery and props

There are big advantages to the camp format, where you are doing sessions every day for a week or two. One advantage is that you have more time with the actors, and they have more time with one another. If the sessions are daily, you do not have to feel as if you are starting over each session. Consistency and carryover are huge benefits. The other benefit is having time to have the actors create scenery and props for their production.

You will need to be very aware of your performance space when having the actors design scenery. It is important for the leaders to have a clear vision of how large the backdrops can and should be, as well as how and to what they will be attached. Once you have those parameters in mind, let the creativity begin. This is a great time to have the actors work together in the creative process. You will have some actors who will tell you they are horrible at art and could not possibly help without messing it up. However, anybody can paint the sky blue or the grass green, right?

First, the actors need to design what they would like the stage to look like for their group scene (see Figures 9.1 and 9.2 for set design sketch form and sample). Remind your actors to use pencil and to have erasers handy because there will be ongoing revisions during this process. You may also want to have extra copies of this form available. Groups can approach this in a couple of different ways. They can sit down together, decide who will be the sketch artist, and give input as a group as he sketches. Some groups have found this approach difficult, and have instead each drawn individual sketches. They then brought the sketches together and decided what should be included in the final sketch. Either way, this is a great exercise in co-operation, problem solving and perspective taking. Actors need to present their ideas, listen to the ideas of their peers, and come up with a final product cooperatively. Some adult facilitation may be needed during this process, but adults should be careful only to facilitate where needed, and to have the actors make the final decisions. They will have to take pride in their final product after this process!

Key skills

✓ Negotiating and compromising
✓ Collaboration
✓ Group decision making

Purchase large rolls of bulletin board paper. It comes in 36" (91.5 cm) and 48" (122 cm) widths and many different lengths. You can buy this at a teacher supply store, from a catalog, or online (www.abcschoolsupply.com or www.becker.com). These places will also have washable tempera paint and brushes. Several packs of markers

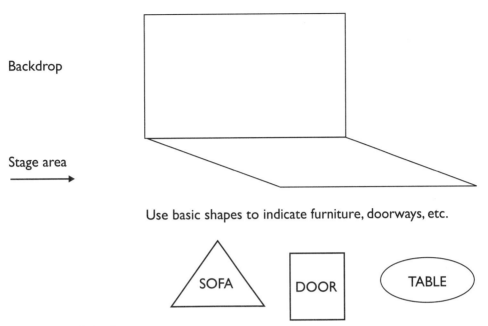

Backdrop

Stage area

Use basic shapes to indicate furniture, doorways, etc.

SOFA   DOOR   TABLE

Figure 9.1 Scenic design form

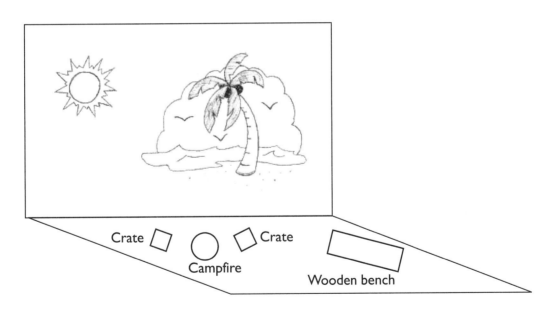

Crate   Campfire   Crate

Wooden bench

Discuss backdrop ideas with group
Create sketches, individually or as a group
Consolidate ideas into one final sketch for the scene's backdrop

Figure 9.2 Example of completed scenic design form

will be needed. Markers are available in "classpacks" if you are going to do lots of groups and need many of each color. Be sure to bring small containers for pouring and mixing paint. The small Glad containers work well and have secure lids so paint can be stored in them overnight. How you set up your painting areas will depend on your space and facility. Ideally, it is great to have several tables together for groups to work on smaller pieces, and a very large drop cloth across the floor for the larger backdrops. One facility required that we do the painting outside because of the floors in the actual space. So we scheduled painting on the days with nice weather. Being flexible is very important, and also gives you the opportunity to teach your actors flexibility!

Costumes and props

Once everyone is familiar with the scenes and they have begun to think about their scenic design, it is time to think about adding props and costumes. Once you have established your program you may begin to collect bits and pieces that you can use repeatedly (see Chapter 4, "Paired Activities"). However, when you begin you should keep it simple. Many of the partner scenes just require everyday clothing that can be found in your actor's closet (or closets of their parents). Have the cast of each scene collaborate on what the characters might wear.

Key skills

✓ Group problem solving
✓ Making and using lists!
✓ Taking responsibility
✓ Working toward a common goal

For some of the scenes that may involve more costuming, be creative. Think about how you can make it simple and yet effective. For example, if you were doing a scene involving animal characters, you could ask the cast to wear a solid color appropriate to the animal. The cat might wear gray or black. The cow could wear brown. A zebra could wear white and you could add stripes with electrical tape. Then headpieces can be made fairly simply. You can use plastic headbands and hot glue on felt ears. Or you could get plain white visors or painter's caps from the craft store and have each actor decorate them accordingly. If you have a budget, you can buy a variety of animal hats from www.orientaltrading.com for a very reasonable price. They have foam animal visors as well as cotton hats.

For other types of characters, you can "suggest" the costume with simple accessories. An old woman may wear a shawl and gloves. A judge can wear someone's graduation robe. A salesman may wear suspenders or a bow tie. A nurse or doctor can wear white. A policeman could wear a blue shirt and a badge made from poster board. Get your actors involved in this discussion and you may come up with some really great ideas.

Some skits may require simple props. Many can be gotten from your home or from one of your actors' homes. This is a great opportunity to teach the actors the power of tools such as a list. That may sound simple, but for many of these young people, learning the skill of making and using a list could have a huge impact on their level of success in high school and beyond (see Figure 9.3). As you brainstorm what costume or prop items will be needed, be sure each actor has a sheet of paper with their name on it. Also have someone make a master list including the names of those who volunteered to bring in items. This would be a great job for someone who wants to be stage manager and focus on more of the "behind the scenes" work. Remind your actors that they need to *ask* before bringing anything from home. It would not be so good if someone brought in his grandmother's heirloom tea set without asking! My experience has been that the actors take great pride in having contributed to the show by bringing in items to use.

Figure 9.3 Sample list

Chapter 10

The "Really Big Show"

Matt

After each show, our audience is called upon to ask questions of the actors. This particular group was younger, and parents asked them what they liked best, how they remembered their lines, and similar questions. Then a young boy of about six years raised his hand. When called upon he said, "I don't have a question. I just wanted to say how proud I am of my big brother, Matt. He did a great job in the show." Sitting on stage, big brother Matt beamed with pride.

Whether you are running a four-week session that meets once a week, or a two-week daily camp, the final showcase is a very important part of theater groups. This is the opportunity for your actors to perform and show what they have learned, and the opportunity for parents and others to discover more about what you are doing. If you share my experience, you will never feel like they are ready for the show, but it always comes together anyway!

So now you are getting closer to the date of the big day, and you need to decide upon a sequence of scenes and activities for the showcase. It is important to set this up so that the actors become familiar with the order of events. The actors will need to know when to change costumes, and when to be ready for an entrance. If this is a camp where you've been able to have the actors create scenery, they will need to know when to move scenery as well. Be sure to post a detailed list of the sequence of activities and scenes and the actors that are involved in each. Be sure to have the actors rehearse the sequence before show time.

It works well to start the showcase by having actors demonstrate some of the warm-up games and activities to the audience. This not only warms up the audience, but also serves to take some of the pressure off your nervous actors. These are familiar activities and there is nothing that requires memorization. Success here will build your actors' level of confidence so they are ready for the more challenging activities. You may want to have an actor explain the function of each activity to the audience. If you plan to do this, let the actor rehearse his answer—again we want to ensure success. Also, keep in mind that we are telling the audience what the function is in terms of *acting*, not in terms of having social deficits. For example, in "Bamboozle," the function of the game in terms of acting is to work on "The Big 3" (see Figure 3.1). Those skills—using body language, facial expressions and vocal tone—are needed in acting in order to portray characters and emotions. For this group, we are also addressing those issues to overcome deficits in social cognition, but they do not need to have that pointed out.

After the demonstrations are complete, you can begin to perform open scenes and then paired scenes. It is effective to close the show with your larger group scenes, especially as they are generally the ones that lend themselves to more scenery and more involved costumes. The "silly skits" are usually real crowd pleasers too!

The program

In the program the names of the cast members should appear in a list. Then you may want to list the warm-up activities that the actors will demonstrate. You do not need to list the actors individually here. List the activities, and put "The Cast" or "The Company." Then list the scenes in the order they will be performed with both the character names and the actor's name listed (see sample pages in Figure 10.1).

Be sure to list any organizations or individuals who donated items, offered support, or in any other way contributed to your program's success. These names can be listed in a category simply titled "Special Thanks." Another popular feature is a page with only the word "Autographs" on it. Encourage the actors to ask other actors to sign their program and perhaps exchange email addresses or phone numbers. You may also find that children and/or grandparents in the audience want the actors to sign their programs. The actors really enjoy that little bit of stardom!

DEMONSTRATIONS

Presented by
The Cast

Name Game

The Power

Bamboozle

Open Scenes

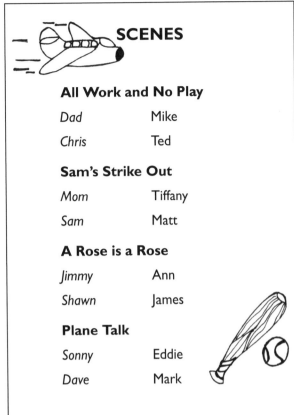

SCENES

All Work and No Play

Dad	Mike
Chris	Ted

Sam's Strike Out

Mom	Tiffany
Sam	Matt

A Rose is a Rose

Jimmy	Ann
Shawn	James

Plane Talk

Sonny	Eddie
Dave	Mark

Figure 10.1 Sample program pages

Chapter 11
It's a Wrap!

Mike

When one new teenage girl joined the teen group, she was extremely nervous. One of my veteran teens, Mike, said to her, "The first time I came, my mom had to drag me here. I didn't want to come. I was so nervous! By the time the first day was over, I was hooked! I couldn't wait to come back."

When the proverbial curtain has come down, and your session is finished, it is my personal guarantee you will have youngsters and parents asking when the next session will occur. Hopefully, you can secure a space so that you can schedule ongoing sessions. In some cases you may need to scout around to see what other locations might work and be willing to house your program. In some cases a non-profit performing arts center or community theater may want to work with you as part of their community service mission. Also, through non-profit organizations, there might be great opportunity to apply for grants so that you can offer scholarships to those who cannot afford private pay, or to fund the program in its entirety.

In any case, once you organize and run your own program, you will continue to fine tune it and mold it to fit both your groups and your personal style. As you do this, please keep in mind the two primary goals of the Acting Antics program:

1. To introduce the youngsters to a leisure time activity in which they can be successful, work with other youngsters, and possibly develop a lifetime interest.

2. To increase the social cognition of the youngsters through a fun, dynamic, interactive program that focuses on the youngsters' strengths in its efforts to improve the deficit areas.

Encourage your school district also to consider this type of program as an Extended School Year option, or as an after-school activity. Although some of these techniques can certainly be used in social skills groups, they are most effective in a more intensive context in which "acting" and being a critical audience member are the focal points.

Carol Gray has said during presentations that the most important things she has learned about autism were learned from individuals who have autism. Truer words could not be found to express my experiences with my actors during these theater workshops. During every session, expect to learn more about how your actors think and what ideas might be added to the program to help them grow. Sometimes their creativity will astound you! This is a journey where the path you follow is as important as the final destination. So jump on, hold the reins, and enjoy the ride!!

The End…less possibilities will amaze you!

Appendix A

Sample Schedules and Activity Lists

Schedule

DAY 1—Teen Group

Sample Day 1 leader's schedule for an adolescent group that meets for 2 hours, once a week, for 5–6 weeks.

6:00 Icebreaker—Introduce "Big 3"

- Review set-up of room
- Review schedule of activities

6:15 Circle Activities

- Actors introduce themselves
- Name Game
- The Power
- Bamboozle

6:45 Actor's Rules

- Review rules and encourage discussion
- See if anyone wants to make a poster

7:00 Flexible Phrases

- Assign partners
- Give one or two phrases to each pair
- Actors work in pairs for five minutes
- Regroup to audience position—each pair performs phrases

7:20 Silly Skit

- Introduce skit
- Assign roles—perform
- Switch roles—perform
- Discuss humor in skit from audience perspective

7:40 Taxi Driver

- Brainstorm and write list of possible characters
- Practice rotation scheme
- Model a round with helpers, more cognizant actors
- Play a round if time allows

7:55 Regroup in Circle

- Announcements
- Preview of next week
- Quick game to close

Schedule

DAY 1—Teen Group

Sample Day 1 schedule for actors, corresponding directly to leader's schedule. You may or may not want to omit the times on the actors' schedule, depending on flexibility of the group.

6:00 Welcome

6:15 Circle Activities
- Name Game
- The Power
- Bamboozle

6:45 Actor's Rules

7:00 Flexible Phrases

7:20 Silly Skit

7:40 Taxi Driver

7:55 Wrap-up

Schedule

DAY 2—Teen Group

Sample Day 1 leader's schedule for an adolescent group that meets for 2 hours, once a week, for 5–6 weeks.

6:00 Review Day's Schedule

Circle Activities

- Name Game
- The Power
- Bamboozle

6:20 Review

- "Big 3"—ask for volunteer to make poster
- Actor's Rules—ask for volunteer to make poster

6:30 Open Scenes

- Assign partners different from session 1
- Give each pair a scene (four lines)
- Instruct to come up with two scenarios for scene

6:45 Regroup to Audience Position

- Have each pair perform scene
- Debrief with audience regarding delivery and how the meaning of the lines change with "Big 3"

7:00 Partner Scenes

- Assign scenes to pairs and/or trios. (These partners will work together on this scene throughout coming sessions)
- Direct actors to go with partner(s) and highlight lines, read through dialogue
- Leaders circulate, listen to readings

7:15 Regroup to Audience Position

- Each pair will do reading of script
- Audience looking for "Big 3"
- Group gives positive feedback to each set of actors

7:40 Taxi Driver (see Day 1 Schedule)

7:55 Regroup

- Announcements
- Closing game: Pass-the-Squeeze game

Schedule

DAY 2—Teen Group

Sample Day 1 schedule for actors, corresponding directly to leader's schedule. You may or may not want to omit the times on the actors' schedule, depending on flexibility of the group.

6:00 Circle Activities

- Name Game
- The Power
- Bamboozle
- Review "Big 3"
- Review Actor's Rules

6:30 Open Scenes

7:00 Partner Scenes

7:40 Taxi Driver

7:55 Wrap-up

Schedule

DAY 1—Youth Group

Sample Day 1 leader's schedule for a 7–12-year-old group that meets for 2 hours, once a week, for 5–6 weeks.

6:00 Icebreaker—Introduce "Big 3"

- Review set-up of room
- Review schedule of activities

6:15 Circle Activities

- Name Game
- Pass-the-Squeeze Game
- Bamboozle

6:30 Actor's Rules

- Review rules and encourage discussion
- See if anyone wants to make a poster

6:45 Movement Activity

- Emotions Walk: actors walk in large circle. Leader calls out emotion and actors walk as if happy, angry, sneaky, etc.

7:00 Flexible Phrases

- Demonstrate delivery of a flexible phrase
- Have actors describe "Big 3" used
- Have volunteers come up and deliver differently

7:20 Silly Skit

- Introduce skit
- Assign roles—perform
- Switch roles—perform
- Discuss humor in skit from audience perspective

7:40 Props Game

- Supply one prop such as a large scarf
- Demonstrate pantomime using it as a different object
- Have actors pantomime using the scarf—audience guesses

7:55 Regroup in Circle

- Announcements
- Preview of next week
- Name Game to close

Schedule

DAY 1—Youth Group

Sample Day 1 schedule for actors, corresponding directly to leader's schedule. Note that specific times are not visible for this younger group.

Welcome

Circle Activities

- Name Game
- Pass-the-Squeeze Game
- Bamboozle

Actor's Rules

Emotions Walk

Flexible Phrases

Silly Skit

Props Game

Wrap-up

Schedule

DAY 2—Youth Group

Sample Day 2 leader's schedule for a 7–12-year-old group that meets for 2 hours, once a week, for 5–6 weeks.

6:00 Circle Activities

- Name Game
- Actors and leaders each tell one thing about themselves
- Introduce The Power
- Bamboozle

6:30 Review

- Actor's Rules
- "Big 3"

6:45 Movement Activity—Heads Up

7:00 Flexible Phrases:

- Review—demonstrate flexible phrase delivered two ways
- Assign phrases to pairs of partners
- Have them work independently with partner(s)
- Leaders circulate and assist

7:15 Regroup to Audience Position

- Each pair performs phrases
- Leader facilitates discussion re "Big 3"

7:30 Introduce Taxi Driver Game

- Assist group in brainstorming "characters" and write on board
- Have students demonstrate what each character might do or say
- Practice rotation for Taxi Driver game
- Do one round of Taxi Driver with students picking character from board

7:55 Regroup in Circle

- Announcements
- Preview of next week
- Name Game to close

Schedule

DAY 2—Youth Group

Sample Day 1 schedule for actors, corresponding directly to above leader's schedule. Note that specific times are not visible for this younger group.

Circle Activities

- Name Game
- Introductions
- The Power
- Bamboozle

Review

- Actor's Rules
- "The Big 3"

Heads Up

Flexible Phrases

Taxi Driver Game

Wrap-up

Scenes from a Hat

These are sample scenarios to be cut out and placed in a hat. Two actors pull one slip from the hat and act out the scenario briefly. The goal is for them to come up with a possible solution to the problem.

John doesn't want to go to his friend Ben's party, but doesn't want to hurt Ben's feelings. He is talking to another friend, Tim, about the problem.

Mary wants her new friend, Jill, to go to the movies with Mary and Beth. Beth really doesn't want Jill to go. Mary and Beth are talking about this.

Fred has left his cell phone somewhere and is in a panic because his parents will be furious. His friend George is trying to help.

Jim is totally frustrated because he lost his homework again! He keeps getting poor grades, just because he loses stuff. He is brainstorming with his friend Megan.

Mike was just harassed by a bigger, older student while he was at his locker. He is very upset and wants to get even. He is talking to his friend Joe.

Melissa is furious at her mom because she took away Melissa's internet privileges because she was talking to guys she doesn't know in chat rooms. She is complaining to her big brother, Ben.

Phrases for "Flexible Phrases"

I don't think so.	Come over here.
No thanks.	What's that?
What did you say?	What is it?
Over here.	How much?
I can't see.	Yeah, right.
Sure.	Not right now.
Maybe I will.	Are you kidding?
No way.	What do you think?
Are you finished?	Really?
Tell me.	Are you scared?
That is bad.	Look at that.
How do you know?	It's over.

Inanimate objects

Remember that in this activity the entire group works together to become the object itself, *not* someone operating or using the object. No sounds allowed!

Christmas tree	book
race car	refrigerator
hot air balloon	jello
scooter	bicycle
popcorn	road
airplane	bridge
table	banana
fire engine	pitcher of water
washing machine	electric fence
traffic light	bleachers
video game	dump truck
flower	computer
train	sliding glass door

S-L-O-W News Day

Suggested item list

broccoli	watermelon	crayons
Kermit the Frog	baby duck	ladybug
spoon	piece of chalk	Barney
rye bread	Patrick	sunflower
baseball cap	shoelace	cheerios
tire	swiss cheese	shovel
telephone book	oatmeal	ruler
bubble gum	jello	toothpaste
orange	paper clip	ghost
ham	Clifford	snowball
newspaper	gluestick	elephant

Character ideas for "Taxi Driver"

cowpoke	"American Idol" contestant
valley girl	elderly person
gangster	rapper
bratty child	S-L-O-W talker
superhero	FAST talker
snobby person	farmer
overly happy guy	WWW wrestler
depressed guy	army guy
bank robber	robot
computer geek	Frankenstein
flower child	werewolf
protester	stuck-up model
paranoid Pete	mathematical genius
jogging enthusiast	ecology enthusiast
bored guy	hyper dude

Appendix B

Photocopiable Forms

Intake/registration form

ACTING WORKSHOP

Actor's name . . . .

Age . . . .

Address . . . .

. . . .

. . . .

Phone: . . . .

Email: . . . .

Actor's interests, hobbies, skills, talents? . . . .

. . . .

Any fears or anxieties we should be aware of? . . . .

. . . .

Allergies/medical/dietary issues? . . . .

. . . .

Top three social issues?   1 . . . .

2 . . . .

3 . . . .

Does your child know his/her diagnosis? Yes . . . . No . . . .

I . . . . (do/do not) give permission to take photos or videotape my
actor during acting class.

Parent signature . . . .

Emergency contact # (cell?) . . . .

Open Scenes template

Write your own open scenes.

Characters	Lines

Characters	Lines

Characters	Lines

Open Scene Analysis

You and your partner have received a script including a set of four lines. You will act out your scene two times. Each time the lines will mean something very different, according to the scenario or situation you have created. You and your partner will portray the different meaning and emotions by using the "Big 3": body language, facial expression, and vocal tone.

Scenario 1:

Where are they and what is going on?

How is character #1 feeling? How can you use the "Big 3" to portray those feelings?

How is character #1 feeling? How can you use the "Big 3" to portray those feelings?

Scenario 2:

What *different* situation are the characters in now?

How is character #1 feeling now? How can you use the "Big 3" to portray those feelings?

How is character #1 feeling now? How can you use the "Big 3" to portray those feelings?

"Sell Your Partner"

Interview form

Family and pets		Hobbies, interests
. . . .		. . . .
. . . .		. . . .
. . . .		. . . .
. . . .		. . . .

Name of partner

. . . .

Favorite places to go		What you're really good at
. . . .		. . . .
. . . .		. . . .
. . . .		. . . .

S-L-O-W News Day planning tool

Object:
Headline:
Anchorman's name:
Weathercaster's headline:
Weathercaster's name:
Sportscaster's headline:
Sportscaster's name:
Traffic guy's headline:
Traffic guy's name:
Tune in next week for:
Name of show or station:

Backdrop design: group brainstorming sheet

Actor	Suggestion

Compromise ideas

Group final decision

Set design template

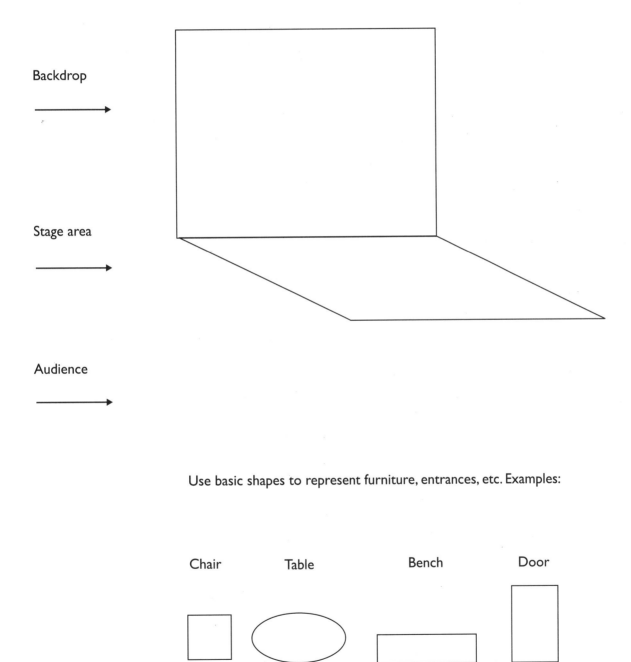

Backdrop

→

Stage area

→

Audience

→

Use basic shapes to represent furniture, entrances, etc. Examples:

Chair   Table   Bench   Door

Actor's Rules

1. Never hurt an actor

2. Listen to the director

"The Big 3"

1. Vocal tone

2. Body language

3. Facial expression

CHEAT OUT

120

PROJECT!

Appendix C

Photocopiable Partner Scripts

Open Scenes

Dan:	How does this thing work?
Casey:	You don't know?
Dan:	You think you can help?

Mr. C:	Good morning, John.
John:	Hi.
Mr. C:	Do you have your homework?

Jude:	What are you doing here?
Joan:	What's going on?
Jude:	You need to get going.

Sandy:	What is he doing over there?
Maria:	I can't believe it.
Sandy:	Do you think we should…?
Maria:	No way.

Open Scenes

Chris:	Hey, cool shirt.
Andy:	Yeah, well I like those sneakers. Where'd you get them, WalMart?
Chris:	Why, you want to get some too?

Man:	What is that?
Pete:	I don't know. I've never seen it before.
Man:	Where did it come from?

Mark:	Are you going tonight?
Sean:	Sure. It should be lots of fun.
Mark:	Yeah, right.
Sean:	I can hardly wait.

Sandy:	Excuse me.
Maria:	Oh, was I in your way?
Sandy:	Just a little.
Maria:	So sorry.

Open Scene: advanced level

Scene I

Bob:	We need to get out of here.
Sam:	Wait a minute.
Bob:	Are you crazy?
Sam:	I have to see.

Bob:	It's on you.
Sam:	I have it covered.
Bob:	Later.
Sam:	I doubt it.

Scenario A

1. Where are they?
2. What is hapening?
3. How does it end?

Scenario B

1. Where are they?
2. What is hapening?
3. How does it end?

Open Scene: advanced level

Scene 2

Ryan:	Naturally.
Val:	Really.
Ryan:	Sure.
Val:	Maybe tomorrow.
Ryan:	Right.

Ryan:	Cool.
Val:	Ya think?
Ryan:	Well?
Val:	No, I can't.

Scenario A

1. Where are they?
2. What is hapening?
3. How does it end?

Scenario B

1. Where are they?
2. What is hapening?
3. How does it end?

Loose Tooth (2 characters)

Mary: Hey Chris. Look! Mom gave me some red crunchy apples!

Chris: Apples! Yum! May I have one please?

Mary: Sure. Here.

Chris: Oh, I forgot. I can't.

Mary: Why not?

Chris: I have a loose tooth.

Mary: A loose tooth? That's great!

Chris: Why is that great?

Mary: That means you are growing up.

Chris: It does? Wow!

Mary: That tooth will come out and a new and bigger tooth will grow in the same place.

Chris: Then…Look out apples. Here I come!!!

Loose Tooth (3 characters)

Mary: Hey everyone! Look what I have! Mom gave me some red crunchy apples!

Ryan: Apples! Yum! May I have one please?

Mary: Sure. There are enough for all of us.

Chris: I can't have one.

Ryan: Why not?

Chris: I have a loose tooth.

Mary: A loose tooth? That's great!

Chris: Why is that great?

Ryan: That means you are growing up.

Chris: It does? Wow!

Mary: That tooth will come out and a new and bigger tooth will grow in the same place.

Ryan: Then you can eat all the apples you want!

Sam's Strike Out (version 1)

Sam: Hey Mom, what's for dinner?

Mom: I really don't know.

Sam: What do you mean? You always have dinner ready at 5:00.

Mom: No dear, not today.

Sam: Oh…OK. Did you get my baseball uniform washed?

Mom: No dear, not today.

Sam: You didn't wash it? Mom, the coach'll kill me! Well, did you get the team snack ready?

Mom: No dear, not today.

Sam: You mean you didn't cut the oranges? Mom, you sure are acting weird. If you did this at your job, you'd get fired.

Mom: You know, it's funny. At my other job…the one I actually get *paid* for…people actually say please and thank you. Try it sometime!

Sam's Strike Out (version 2)

Sam: Hey Mom, what's for dinner?

Mom: I really don't know.

Sam: What do you mean? You always have dinner ready at 5:00.

Mom: Not today.

Sam: Oh…OK. Did you get my baseball uniform washed? This is going to be one sweet game tonight. We'll crush West!

Mom: I think your uniform is right where you left it…in a pile on the floor of your bedroom.

Sam: You didn't wash it? Mom, the coach'll kill me if I show up with grass stains and Pepsi all over my uniform.

Mom: Well, the washer is down the hall on your left. There's soap on the shelf and a cute little knob on the right that turns it on.

Sam: Mom, you sure are acting weird.

Mom: I don't know why you would say that, dear.

Sam: Oh! And I have to bring the team snack for the game today. Dad said you would get the oranges ready and stuff.

Mom: The oranges are in the fridge. The knife is in the drawer, and the Tupperware is in the cabinet.

Sam: You mean you didn't cut them up? I'll never be ready on time! Mom, why are you being like this? If you did this at your job, you'd get fired.

Mom: You know, it's funny. At my other job…the one I actually get *paid* for…people actually say please and thank you. Try it sometime!

A Ghostly Tale

Dean: Hey, do you believe in ghosts?

Sandy: Nah, how about you, Ryan?

Ryan: No, that's stuff my brother says to scare me.

Dean: I'm not so sure. I saw something the other night and it sure looked like a ghost.

Sandy: What are you talking about?

Ryan: What did it look like?

Dean: Well it was big and white and sort of see-through, and it kept saying Deeeeeeean…Deeeean…

Sandy: What did you do?

Ryan: Were you scared?

Dean: Yeah! Wouldn't you be?

Sandy: Well, yeah, I'd be scared!

Ryan: What happened next?

Dean: I woke up!! Ha, ha ha! Gotcha!!

Sandy: Oh, man!

Ryan: Why do we listen to you?!

Oh, Brother!

Nicky: Hey, get out of my room. What do you think you're doing?

Joe: I was just…

Nicky: Well get out. You're not allowed in here.

Joe: Geez, you don't have to yell. I didn't touch anything.

Nicky: I don't care. You're just a pain…now get out.

Joe: Man, I was just going to…

Nicky: You were just going to leave is what you mean.

Joe: Well, OK. Never mind, then.

Nicky: Never mind what?

Joe: Never mind leaving your birthday present on your bed. Think I'll just keep it.

Nicky: Well, I guess I blew that!

Playdate (2 characters)

Chris: Hi Randy. What do you want to play?

Randy: Let's play with Lego!

Chris: No way. How about we ride bikes?

Randy: I don't want to. I want to play with Lego.

Chris: But you always want to do that.

Randy: Well, it's fun building stuff.

Chris: You're no fun!

Randy: Fine, I'm going home!

Chris: Wait Randy. How about if we play Lego first, and *then* ride bikes.

Randy: It's a deal!

Playdate (3 characters)

Chris: Hey guys, what do you want to do?

Sean: I don't know. What do you want to do?

Randy: Let's play with Lego. There's this cool monster I want to build.

Chris: No, I don't want to do that. Let's ride bikes.

Sean: I like to ride bikes *and* do Lego. Which should we do first?

Randy: Lego! I'm really good at building stuff.

Chris: I want to ride bikes! My bike is brand new!

Sean: Can't we do both things?

Randy: Yeah, I guess. Since you want to ride your new bike, maybe we should do that first.

Chris: Thanks Randy!! That would be cool. I promise we'll play Lego after that. I want to see that monster you are talking about!

Sean: That sounds like a good plan guys. Let's go!

A Rose is a Rose is a Rose

Jimmy: Hey, what are you doing?

Shawn: Just reading a book. Why do you look so nervous?

Jimmy: Uhh…nothing really.

Shawn: Yeah right. What did you do?

Jimmy: I kinda, sorta ruined the flowerbed.

Shawn: Oh my gosh, Mom's gonna flip.

Jimmy: The thing is…it's not our flowerbed.

Shawn: What? Whose is it?

Jimmy: Mrs. Johnson's across the street…I fell into her rose bushes. It was an accident, I swear!

Shawn: OH MY GOSH! Her prize roses?! Well, did you tell her?

Jimmy: No, I'm scared. She'll be all mad.

Shawn: She'll be madder if you don't tell.

Jimmy: I can't! I can't!

Shawn: Tell you what. I'll go with you. Better to tell her now and get it over with.

Jimmy: I guess you're right? Can I stand behind you?

Lesson from the Coach

by Susan March

Roy: [*Roy walks into the football coach's office.*] Coach, did you want to see me?

Coach: Yes, Roy. Close the door and sit down.

Roy: Sir, I know you're disappointed with me. I shouldn't have fumbled that ball in the third quarter. We might have won the game if it weren't for me.

Coach: Roy, we're not here to talk about the fumble…

Roy: Then it must have been that missed pass in the fourth. I almost had it…if only I had been a little faster…It makes me so angry!

Coach: No, Roy, I didn't ask you here to talk about the fumble, the missed pass, or even last night's game. We're here to talk about your future.

Roy: Do you want me to sit out the next game? I deserve it.

Coach: Roy, be quiet and just listen! I've known you since PeeWee football days and I've watched you develop into a fine player. You're a hard worker, you take direction well, and you're a natural athlete. The trouble is…You spend as much energy beating yourself up as you do going after our opponents.

Roy: I just want to be the best football player I can be…But then I go and make mistakes like last Friday night.

Coach: Roy, everyone makes mistakes. The important thing is that you learn from them and go on. Every game is a new game. Football is just like the rest of life. You make mistakes, you pick yourself up, think about how you're going to do it differently, and move ahead.

Roy: Then you're not disappointed with me?

Coach: Just the opposite! I called you in here Roy for a couple of reasons. You've shown me that you have the makings of a real leader. A leader inspires by example. I want you to work on using your mistakes to help you learn to be a better player…so that next year, as team captain, you'll inspire the others to do the same.

Roy: Team captain? Me?

Coach: You're my man! Now go back to practice and show me I made the right decision!

Reproduced with permission from Susan March

Enough Already!

Terry: Hey, Randy. What's up? Why the long face?

Randy: I'm kind of bummed out.

Joe: What's the matter?

Randy: My younger brother.

Terry: Your younger brother bums you out? My brother usually just makes me mad!

Joe: Mine just drives me crazy!

Randy: I'm just sick of how he always does everything right. My mom and dad are always talking about how great he is.

Joe: In what ways?

Randy: Oh, he gets all good grades, is on all the sports teams, and does volunteer work, has all these friends. He never does anything wrong!

Terry: Sounds like someone's a little jealous…what's that all about?

Joe: Yeah, Randy, what do you have to be jealous of?

Terry: You shouldn't compare yourself to your brother, man.

Randy: I know what you're saying, but I still get sick of hearing how great he is.

Joe: But what about all the cool stuff YOU do?

Randy: Like what?

Terry: Like walking your little sisters home every day. When we ask you to hang out with us after school, you always do the responsible thing and take them home first.

Joe: You even act like you *like* the little brats! [*Smiles and nudges Randy.*]

Terry: And you're great at all that science stuff ! How do you remember all that stuff anyway?

Randy: I don't know…science seems easy to me, but math drives me nuts.

Terry: And you and me…we're the KINGS of video games!

Randy: I can't argue with you there!

Terry: I'll make you a deal…you help me with the science project, and I'll help you with the math homework!

Joe: And you can both help me beat that video game!

Randy: It's a deal!

Plane Talk

Sonny: Hey, Dave. What's up?

Dave: [*Reading magazine.*] Well, I was just reading about these World War II planes…it is so cool! Do you want to see some of these pictures?

Sonny: Actually I kind of wanted to talk to you. I'm having a tough time at home right now.

Dave: I'm sure it'll be fine. Hey! Look at this one…sweet! Don't ya think?

Sonny: Yeah, it's pretty cool, but I really wish you'd talk to me a minute.

Dave: Well, what is it?

Sonny: It's my folks. My mom just told me they're getting a divorce. I can't believe it. I really thought they would get back together.

Dave: [*Still reading magazine.*] Well, they've been separated a while. It can't be that much of a surprise. Oh baby! Look at the wings on this one!

Sonny: But I have to make some big decisions. They want ME to decide where I should live.

Dave: That's cool. Hey, I'm going to an air show at the airforce base on Saturday…Wanna go?

Sonny: Are you listening to anything I am saying?

Dave: Yo…what's wrong with YOU?

Sonny: I am really freakin' out here, and need somebody to talk to. You're my best friend, and all you want to do is talk about your stupid planes!

Dave: [*Gets up closing magazine.*] Now just a darn minute! Don't call my planes stupid!

Sonny: Never mind, I can see you're too busy. I'll catch you later… [*Starts to leave.*]

Dave: [*Calling after him.*] Hey Sonny you still didn't tell me if you can go Saturday!!

Sonny: Forget it, FRIEND!

Dave: [*Sitting back down with magazine.*] Wonder what's buggin' him?!

Wrestling with a Problem

Sonny: Hey, Dave. What's up?

Dave: [*Reading magazine.*] I was just reading this wrestling magazine…it is so cool! Do you want to see?

Sonny: Actually I kind of wanted to talk to you. I'm having a tough time at home right now.

Dave: I'm sure it'll be fine. Hey! Look at this guy…yo!

Sonny: Yeah, pretty cool, but I really wish you'd talk to me a minute.

Dave: Well, what is it?

Sonny: It's my folks. My mom just told me they're getting a divorce. I can't believe it. I really thought they would get back together.

Dave: [*Still reading magazine.*] Well, it can't be that much of a surprise. Oh, baby! Look at the muscles on this dude!

Sonny: But I have to make some big decisions. They want ME to decide where I should live.

Dave: That's cool. Hey, I'm going to a match on Saturday…Wanna go?

Sonny: Are you listening to anything I am saying?

Dave: Yo…what's wrong with YOU?

Sonny: I am really freakin' out here, and need somebody to talk to. You're my best friend, and all you want to do is talk about your stupid magazine!

Dave: [*Gets up closing magazine.*] Now just a darn minute! Don't call my magazine stupid!

Sonny: Never mind, I can see you're too busy. I'll catch you later…[*Starts to leave.*]

Dave: [*Calling after him.*] Hey Sonny, you still didn't tell me if you can go Saturday!!

Sonny: Forget it, FRIEND!

Dave: [*Sitting back down with magazine.*] Wonder what's buggin' him?!

A Friend in Need

Sonya: Hey, Maria. What's up?

Maria: [*Reading magazine.*] Well, I was just reading Brad and Angelina, and you just can't believe what Jennifer did!

Sonya: Actually I kind of wanted to talk to you. I'm having a tough time at home right now.

Maria: I'm sure it'll be fine. Hey! Look at what she's wearing here. What was she *thinking*?

Sonya: Yeah, it's pretty strange, but I really wish you'd talk to me a minute.

Maria: Well, what is it?

Sonya: It's my folks. My mom just told me they're getting a divorce. I can't believe it. I really thought they would get back together.

Maria: [*Still reading magazine.*] Well, they've been separated a while. It can't be that much of a surprise. Oh, baby! Look at the muscles on this hotty!

Sonya: But I have to make some big decisions. They want ME to decide where I should live.

Maria: That's cool. Hey, I'm going to the mall with the gang Friday night… Wanna go?

Sonya: Are you listening to anything I am saying?

Maria: Yo…what's wrong with YOU?

Sonya: I am really freakin' out here, and need somebody to talk to. You're my best friend, and all you want to do is talk about your stupid gossip magazine!

Maria: [Gets up closing magazine.] Now just a darn minute! Don't call my magazine stupid!

Sonya: Never mind, I can see you're too busy. I'll catch you later… [*Starts to leave.*]

Maria: [*Calling after her.*] Hey, Sonya you still didn't tell me if you can go Friday night!!

Sonya: Forget it, FRIEND!

Maria: [*Sitting back down with magazine.*] Wonder what's buggin' her?!

The Day of the Jacket

Mary: [*Has new wild jacket.*] Surprise! What do you think?

Jim: Oh, yeah…new jacket. [*Trying to be diplomatic.*]

Mary: Yeah! Do you like it?

Jim: I've…I've never seen anything quite like it. Honest! Not since… *Joseph and the Technicolor Dreamcoat*!

Mary: But do you *like* it?

Jim: Well… think it's…*um*…*the* important thing is…do YOU like it?

Mary: It's way cool…but I think it needs some work.

Jim: [*Hopefully.*] You do???

Mary: Yeah, it's still a little too ordinary for me.

Jim: Oh.

Mary: But I want to look good for you. You're the one who has to look at it every time we go out.

Jim: [*Under his breath.*] You could always wear something over it.

Mary: What did you say?

Jim: I said…I just can't get over it!

Mary: So you like it. It's important that you like it.

Jim: Oh…"like" doesn't capture my feelings.

Mary: Good, 'cause here's a present for you.

Jim: What's that?

Mary: Open it!

Jim: OK?

Mary: Yeah, that's why I wanted to make sure you liked my jacket. It's a "his and her's" style! Yours is on layaway…c'mon!

Jim: [*Groans as Mary drags him offstage.*]

The Conversation

by Susan March

Brian: I'm going to visit my grandparents in Pittsburgh this weekend.

Mark: What are you going to do?

Brian: I think my grandfather is going to take me to a cave nearby called Crystal Cave.

Chris: [*Chiming in.*] Did you know that most caves are made when underground water dissolves limestone or marble? The water that trickles down through the ground has carbon dioxide in it. That makes an acid in the water that eats away at the rock…

Brian: What…?

Chris: [*Continuing.*] The water may drop below the cave or an earthquake may lift the cave up. Then air fills up the cave. The rock above the cave might collapse and form a sink hole entrance. Some caves are formed by lava from a volcano…

Mark: Chris…?

Chris: The longest cave ever explored is in Kentucky. It's more than 190 miles long. Some caves have underground lakes, rivers and waterfalls. Did you ever hear of a stalagmite? That's a formation that looks like a cone on the floor of the cave. It's formed by water dripping from the roof of a cave…

Brian: A what?

Chris: And then there's the stalactite. It sounds a little like stalagmite but it has a "t" in it. It looks like an icicle hanging from the roof of the cave. It's formed by dripping water that contains lime. That's not the kind of lime that you eat. Some cave explorers found stalactites as thin as straws. Do you know what they call cave exploring? It's called spelunking.

Mark: Oh, brother… [*Brian and Mark look at each other, rolling their eyes.*]

Chris: My brother and I went spelunking in West Virginia. We…

[*Mark and Brian pick up their trays and leave the table.*]

Chris: [*Looking puzzled.*] Hey, where are you going? I'm not done! [*Sighs.*] Oh well, I guess what they say is right. The art of conversation is dead!

Reproduced with permission from Susan March

The Bully

by Susan March

[*Greg and Matt are walking in the hallway at school. Jake passes by with one of his buddies and calls out to Greg.*]

Jake: Hey, you [*Looking at Greg.*]…what a chicken brain! What are you doing in this school? You belong in kindergarten…ha, ha.

Greg: [*Visibly upset.*]You…you're a chicken brain!

Jake: What…you can't even think for yourself? [*Makes chicken noises, laughs, and exits offstage. Circles around for re-entry later.*]

Greg: [*To Matt.*] He makes me so angry I could spit!

Matt: I know. He really has power over you. But, after all, you gave it to him.

Greg: What do you mean? I didn't give him anything!

Matt: Sure you did. Every time you show him he is making you mad, it makes him feel powerful. He knows he can get a reaction from you.

Greg: Well you'd feel the same way if he teased you like that…in front of everyone in the school!

Matt: He used to…but I made him stop.

Greg: How did you do that?

Matt: I just ignored him…pretended he didn't exist. Eventually he stopped teasing me. It wasn't fun for him anymore.

Greg: I don't think I could do that.

Matt: Sure you could. Try it next time. Oh…it looks like next time is coming sooner than we thought. [*Jake is walking down the hall towards the boys.*]

Jake: Hey, chicken brain…looking for your chicken feed? Ha, ha!

Greg: [*Ignoring Jake.*] Matt, do you want to go to see the Batman movie with me this weekend? I hear it's playing at the Regal now.

Jake: I said…chicken brain…where's your pen?

Matt: [*Ignoring Jake.*] Sure. Maybe you could come over to my house for pizza first.

[*Jake shrugging his shoulders and looking in another direction, calling out to someone off stage as he walks off stage.*]

Jake: Andy…yeah, you with the turkey legs…I saw you running in gym today…more like waddling! Ha, ha, ha!

Greg: [*To Matt.*] I guess we'd better have a talk with Andy.

[*Matt nods and the boys exit together.*]

Reproduced with permission from Susan March

Kool Kat

Kat: Hey, you're new here aren't you?

Anna: Yeah, I'm Anna.

Kat: Hi Anna. I'm Kathy, but you can call me "Kat." Let's sit over here and I can give you the scoop about Medford Middle School.

Anna: OK, Kat.

Kat: Now, you always want to sit at this table, because this is where the cool girls always sit.

Anna: So it's just a wild guess, but I suppose you're a "cool girl."

Kat: Of course! Next, I saw you earlier talking to Mandi, that girl who's in the band. You *really* don't want to be seen with the band geeks.

Anna: You're kidding, right?

Kat: Oh no. You have to remember that image is everything!

Anna: Wow, that's deep.

Kat: Yes, well, I heard you're kinda smart too, but be careful not to show it too much. You don't want to be identified with the nerds.

Anna: So your advice is not to act too smart.

Kat: Yeah, and only join the cool clubs, like the fashion club or cheer-leading or the pep club. Things like chess club and computer club are full of those nerds.

Anna: Wow, you certainly seem to have things figured out, don't you?

Kat: And the rapper dudes over there—keep away. They only like you if you like their music. They're so judgmental.

Anna: And the "cool girls" are not judgmental?

Kat: Oh no, we just know what's cool! So are you ready to meet the "cool girls?"

Anna: No, not right now. I have to go pick up my flute before I go to the library and then to computer club. Oh, [*Taking out headphones.*] and I think I will listen to some rap on the way. Later, oh cool one.

Kat: Geez, you just can't be nice to some people.

Shy Guy

Damon: Hey, John…so, did you talk to Laura yet?

John: No, she doesn't want to talk to me.

Damon: How do you know that if you don't even try?

John: Well, she's so smart and pretty, and I'm just a nobody.

Damon: Look, first of all you're not a nobody. You are a smart, interesting person. And you don't have to ask her out or anything, just talk to her.

John: I don't know what to talk to her about.

Damon: Well, you guys do have some things in common. You're both in the band, for example. And I know you love animals and Laura is always talking about her dogs.

John: Oh that's cool. Wow, I wonder what kind of dogs she has.

Damon: That's what you should ask her, Einstein.

John: Oh, yeah. I could probably do that.

Damon: That's the spirit. Just start a casual conversation and see what happens.

John: What if she tells me to get lost?

Damon: Well, if she's that rude, I'm thinking you probably don't need her for a friend.

John: I guess that's true.

Damon: But I really can't see her doing that. So just give it a shot.

John: I guess.

Damon: You guess? What's your problem? What could possibly go wrong?

John: Lots of things. I could forget what I wanted to say and stand there looking like a dope. Or I could call her the wrong name and then I would have to crawl under the nearest piece of furniture and hide!

Damon: Man, you are one stressed out dude. Will you just relax? Just go up to her in study hall, say hi, and start a conversation, You are not asking her to marry you or anything! Now study hall starts in three minutes, so you'd better get going.

John: Now? You want me to do it now? I can't do that. I'm not ready. I'll mess it up. She'll hate me!

Damon: Man, you're hopeless. Why do I keep on trying?

John: Because you're my best friend, that's why.

Damon: Yeah, I guess, but I'm sure not getting anywhere with you.

John: You know what? I'm going to do it. You have confidence in me so I should have confidence in myself too. What could it hurt? I am definitely planning to talk to Laura. Tomorrow…I will talk to Laura tomorrow. Or Thursday at the latest. [*Starts walking offstage.*]

Damon: Oh brother. [*Follows John offstage, shaking his head.*]

Cool or Fool?

Chad: Hey, Mark, what's up?

Mark: Not much. How about you?

Chad: Well, the guys and I were wondering if you want to go to the movies with the gang tonight?

Mark: Well, yeah, that'd be cool. What time?

Chad: Whoa, wait a minute. Slow down. First the guys want to be sure you're one of the guys, ya know what I mean?

Mark: No, I don't understand. What do you mean?

Chad: Well, to be one of the guys, you kind of have to prove yourself.

Mark: OK, that's cool. What do I need to do?

Chad: Well, you know the mini-mart down on the corner of Main Street?

Mark: Yeah, the one next to the diner.

Chad: Yeah, that's the one. The rest of the guys are going to meet us there.

Mark: OK. Why are we meeting at the mini-mart?

Chad: Well, the guys are hungry and we don't have the money to buy the pricey movie house stuff, so Joe and Luke and I thought you could go and get some candy bars from the mini-mart.

Mark: But I barely have enough money to get in the movie.

Chad: We don't want you to buy it, dork, we want you to lift it. You know…a five-finger discount.

Mark: You've got to be kidding. You want me to steal candy for you guys?

Chad: Yeah, just three candy bars…four if you want one. No biggie.

Mark: Why don't we just go see the movie, and then you guys can come back to my house and get something to eat?

Chad: You don't get it do you, dude? It's not just the candy. The guys need to know that you aren't a scared little wimp, that you would take a risk for them. It's kind of an initiation.

Mark: I don't know…I've never stolen anything.

Chad: No time like the present. C'mon, let's go.

Mark: I'm not sure I want to hang out with you guys if stealing is what it takes.

Chad: C'mon. I stood up for you! The other guys didn't think you would do it, but I told them you would be cool with it.

Mark: [*Sarcastically.*] Sorry to…uh…let you down, but hanging with a bunch of losers who want you to steal for them isn't my thing.

Chad: Forget it. The guys were right. You're a loser. [*Walks off.*]

Mark: I can't believe I thought those guys were cool. I wonder how cool they'll feel when they end up in juvey hall! Talk about losers!

Appendix D

Group Scripts

The King's Royal Papers

Punchline script for flexible number of actors. Script is suitable for actors who are readers and/or non-readers.

King is seated on throne in middle of stage. Herald stands to his right.

King whispers angrily to Herald.

Herald trumpets [*kazoo*] and announces: "The King demands his royal papers!"

Queen enters nervously from left, kneels, presents paper* to King.

He looks at it, sneers, throws it to ground. Queen runs off stage right, crying.

Herald trumpets [*kazoo*] and announces: "The King demands his royal papers!"

Subsequent individuals** or groups enter, each presenting the King with some variation of paper.* He inspects and then throws it to ground. Each person runs off in fear as the King is getting angrier and angrier.

The last person to enter is the Jester. He holds a velvet pillow on which there is a roll of toilet paper. He enters timidly. The King stands, staring. The King motions him forward. The King grabs and hugs the Jester, taking the roll of paper. The King holds the paper up in triumph, then runs offstage right.

The Jester and Herald look at one another and then out to audience saying: "When ya gotta go, ya gotta go!!"

* On the first entrance the paper should be something that looks like a scroll or parchment. Then as each group enters, the paper becomes less and less believable for the error. For example, you could use bright pink construction paper, wallpaper, newspaper. Once we had a knight enter with a carton of computer copy paper. Have fun with it!

** Suggested characters include pages, knights, princess, ladies in waiting, and townsfolk.

Is It Time Yet?

Punchline script for flexible number of actors. Script is suitable for actors who are readers and/or non-readers.

Actors are seated, side by side, on chairs or on a bench.

Each has right leg crossed over left knee.

Each is holding a hardcover book as if reading it.

Actor on audience far right turns to actor on his right and asks: "Is it time yet?"

That actor turns to next actor and asks same question.

This continues until the final actor on left is asked: "Is it time yet?"

Final actor replies: "No it isn't time" to the actor on his or her left.

Each actor passes the response to next actor until it reaches first actor.

First actor sighs and returns attention to book.

Five seconds later he turns to actor on his right and asks: "Is it time yet?"

The entire process is repeated until the final actor is asked.

This time he or she looks at watch and says: "Yes, it's time."

This response is passes down the line to the original actor.

In perfect unison the actors:

1.   Close book.

2.   Put right leg down.

3.   Put left leg up.

4.   Open book and resume reading.

Grub's On!

Scene: *A campfire out on the prairie. Joe, the cook of the group, is stirring a big pot.*

Joe: Grub's ON!!!

Cowboy 1:   Hey, Joe…this plate is filthy!

Joe: Hey, camper! That plate is as clean as Three Rivers can git it. Sit down and eat!

Cowboy 2:   Yo, Joe…You expect me to drink outa this cup?

Joe: Relax cowboy! It's as clean as Three Rivers can git it.

Cowboy 3:   This is gross, Joe. Don't you ever warsh the silver?

Cowboy 4:   OR the plates, or yer hands even?

Joe: Like I told the others…it's as clean as Three Rivers can git it.

Cowboy 5:   Any of you boys ever seen Joe warsh this stuff down at the river?

Joe: Here boy…here boy! [*Dog enters, Joe lays plates down and dog begins to lick them.*] There you go, Three Rivers. See how clean you kin get 'em this time!

Cowboys: [*All grab stomachs and run off.*] Agh!!!

Order in the Court (5 characters)

Scene: *Courtroom. Judge is behind desk. Two policemen escort man into courtroom. Judge pounds gavel twice.*

Judge: *[Pounds gavel.]* Order in the court! First case please!

Policeman: Your honor, this man was caught throwing pebbles into the lake! *[Policeman enters with prisoner.]*

Judge: That's despicable!! Give that man 30 days in jail! *[Policeman exits with prisoner.]*

Reporter: Ladies and gentlemen, I can't believe it. The judge just gave this man 30 days for throwing pebbles!?! Stay tuned…

Judge: Order in the court! Next case please!

Policeman: Your honor, now THIS man was caught throwing pebbles into the lake. *[Escorting another man into court.]*

Judge: Unbelievable! Give that man 30 days in jail! *[Pounds gavel one time.]*

Reporter: I really can't believe this…The judge just gave another man 30 days for throwing pebbles!?! No wonder they call him the HANGING judge!

Judge: Quiet in the courtroom! Order! Order!

Girl: *[Soaking wet.]* Hi, I've just come from the lake. My name is Pebbles.

Order in the Court (7 characters)

Scene: *Courtroom. Judge is behind desk. Two policemen escort man into courtroom. Judge pounds gavel twice.*

Bailiff: Will the court please come to order? First case please!!

Judge: What is this man accused of?

Policeman 1: [*Escorting prisoner.*] He was throwing pebbles in the lake!

Policeman 2: And it isn't the first time, either!

Judge: That's disgraceful! Give that man 30 days in jail! [*Policemen exit with prisoner.*]

Reporter 1: I can't believe that! He gave him 30 days for throwing pebbles!?!

Reporter 2: He's some tough judge!

Judge: Quiet in the courtroom!

Bailiff: Next case please!!!

Policeman 1: Got another one your honor! [*Escorting another man into court.*]

Policeman 2: Yep…throwing pebbles into the lake!

Judge: That's disgraceful! Give that man 30 days in jail! [*Pounds gavel one time.*]

Reporter 1: I really can't believe this.

Reporter 2: Me neither…30 days for throwing pebbles!!

Judge: Order! Quiet in the courtroom!

Girl: [*Soaking wet.*] Hi, I've just come from the lake. My name is Pebbles.

Order in the Court (9 characters)

Scene: *Courtroom. Judge is behind desk. Two policemen escort man into courtroom. Judge pounds gavel three times.*

Bailiff: Will the court please come to order? First case please!!

Judge: What is this man accused of?

Policeman 1:   [*Escorting prisoner.*] He was throwing pebbles in the lake!

Policeman 2:   And it isn't the first time, either!

Man 1:   Your honor, they've got the wrong guy!

Judge: Quiet! That's disgraceful! Give this man 30 days in jail! [*Policemen exit with prisoner.*]

Reporter 1:   Breaking news! The judge gave the man 30 days just for throwing pebbles!?!

Reporter 2:   Stay tuned for further developments.

Judge: Quiet in the courtroom!

Bailiff: Yes, quiet in the courtroom! Next case please!!!

Policeman 1:   Got another one your honor! [*Escorting another man into court.*]

Policeman 2:   Yep…throwing pebbles into the lake!

Man 2:   I'm innocent I tell ya! I been framed!

Judge: QUIET, YOU!!! Your behavior is disgraceful! Give this man 30 days in jail! [*Pounds gavel one time.*]

Reporter 1:   I really can't believe this, folks! I have never seen such a thing!

Reporter 2:   Me neither…30 days for throwing pebbles!! Unbelievable! Back to you, Tom.

Judge: Order! Order! Quiet in the courtroom!

Policeman 2:   Excuse me your honor. This young lady would like a word with you.

Girl: [*Soaking wet.*] Hello, your honor. I've just come from the lake. My name is Pebbles.

Trouble (4 characters)

Shut Up: Hi. My name's Shut Up and this is my dog Trouble. [*Looking around.*] Trouble!! Here, Trouble! I sure hope Trouble's OK. Well, I'd better get to school.

Teacher: Well, what is your name?

Shut Up: Shut up.

Teacher: Excuse me! I asked you your name!

Shut Up: Shut Up.

Teacher: You rude young man! You will need to go see the Dean of Students!

Dean: Well, what is your name?

Shut Up: Shut Up!

Dean: I beg your pardon! WHAT IS YOUR NAME??

Shut Up: Shut Up!

Dean: Well I never…! I will need to send you to the Principal!

Principal: So what is your name, young man?

Shut Up: Shut Up!

Principal: Shut up is it?!! Are you looking for TROUBLE?!!

Shut Up: As a matter of fact I am! Have you seen him?

Trouble (6 characters)

Shut Up: Hi. My name's Shut Up and this is my dog Trouble.

Dog: Ruff, ruff, ruff!

Boy: What kind of crazy names are those? [*Dog runs off.*]

Shut Up: They are not crazy names!

Boy: OK, whatever you say!

Shut Up: [*Looking around.*] Trouble!! Here, Trouble! I sure hope Trouble's OK. Well, I'd better get to school.

Teacher: Well, what is your name?

Shut Up: Shut Up.

Teacher: Excuse me! I asked you your name!

Shut Up: Shut Up.

Teacher: You rude young man! You will need to go see the Dean of Students!

Dean: Well, what is your name?

Shut Up: Shut Up!

Dean: I beg your pardon! WHAT IS YOUR NAME??

Shut Up: Shut Up!

Dean: Well I never…! I will need to send you to the Principal!

Principal: So what is your name, young man?

Shut Up: Shut Up.

Principal: Shut up is it?!! Are you looking for TROUBLE?!!

Shut Up: As a matter of fact I am! Have you seen him?

The Viper (6 characters)

Bernie Bigshot: Sure is nice to be the boss and tell everyone else what to do. [*Puts feet up on desk.*]

Irma Staples: [*Answers phone.*] Bernie Bigshot's office. Who?… What?… When?… [*Hangs up.*] Oh My! [*Says to Mr. Cooler.*] I just got a call. The viper is coming!!

Mr. Poindexter Pen: When?? NOW?? I'm not ready!!! [*Turns to boss.*] I hate to tell you BOSS, but the viper is coming!

Bernie Bigshot: [*Getting up.*] What are you talking about?

Ida Whiner: Mr. Bigshot…I have just heard that today is the day that the viper is coming. Tell me it isn't true!

Irma Staples: I'm afraid it is true, Ida. [*Ida blows nose and cries. Others chatter nervously.*]

Mr. Broomall: [*Enters sweeping floor.*] I don't know what all the fuss is about…you knew he was coming sooner or later.

Mr. Bigshot: [*Looks at everyone shaking and fussing.*] Now. Everyone…we must remain calm…after all it's only the viper. [*Silent pause. All look at him wide eyed.*] The VIPER! AGH!! [*All, including Mr. B, start running around screaming and fussing.*]

Viper: [*Enters with bucket, squeegee and rag. All stop in their tracks to look at him. Mr. B is under desk.*] Haylo. I am Valter the Viper, the vindow viper. I've come to vipe your vindows!! [*All workers sigh in relief.*]

Bernie Bigshot: [*Sneaking out from under desk, brushing self off—quietly says.*] I knew that, yes, I knew that.

[*Workers all look at him with "Yeah right!" look.*]

The Viper (8 characters)

Bernie Bigshot: Sure is nice to be the boss and tell everyone else what to do. [*Puts feet up on desk.*]

Mr. Teller Phone: [*Answers phone*] Bernie Bigshot's office…Who?… What?… When?… [*Hangs up.*] Oh My! [*Says to Mr. Cooler.*] I just got a call. The viper is coming!!

Mr. Walter Cooler: No, you can't mean it? Oh no! [*Turns to Mr. Pen.*] The viper is coming…do you believe it??

Mr. Poindexter Pen: When?? NOW?? I'm not ready!!! [*Turns to Ms. Staples.*] I hate to tell you but the viper is coming!

Mr. Broomall: [*Enters sweeping floor.*] I don't know what all the fuss is about…you knew he was coming sooner or later.

Irma Staples: It can't be true! [*Turns to Mr. Copy.*] Mr. Copy…they are telling me the viper is coming today. Tell me it isn't so… [*Blows nose loudly into hankie.*]

Mr. Forman Copy: [*GASP!*] Oh no, I'd better let the boss know…here goes nothing. [*To Mr. Bigshot.*] Mr. Bigshot…I have just learned that today is the day that the viper is coming.

Bernie Bigshot: [*Looks at everyone shaking and fussing.*] Now. Everyone…we must remain calm…after all it's only the viper. [*Silent pause. All look at him wide eyed.*] The VIPER! AGH!! [*All, including Mr. B, start running around screaming and fussing.*]

Viper: [*Enters with bucket, squeegee and rag. All stop in their tracks to look at him. Mr. B is under desk.*] Haylo. I am Valter the Viper, the vindow viper. I've come to vipe your vindows!! [*All workers sigh in relief.*]

Bernie Bigshot: [*Sneaking out from under desk, brushing self off—quietly says.*] I knew that, yes, I knew that.

[*Workers all look at him with "Yeah right!" look.*]

Stranded on a Desert Island

This scene can be done with as few as four or as many as 12+ characters. You can do the lines as written, or you can have each actor come up with one thing they would miss the most if stranded on an island, and replace the items in the script with their personal preferences.

Scene: *All actors are in tattered clothing, pacing around the "island" looking hot, thirsty, and tired. After each "wish" there should be a sound effect, light flickering, and the actor spins off the stage as if his or her wish was magically granted.*

Person 1:   Geez, I sure wish I was home with a 20-ounce Pepsi! [*Disappears.*]

Person 2:   I wish I was in a nice cool swimming pool! [*Disappears.*]

Person 3:   I wish I was at the deli eating an extra long Italian sub! [*Disappears.*]

Person 4:   I wish I were at the mall shopping, shopping, shopping! [*Disappears.*]

Person 5:   I wish I was laying on the beach soaking up some rays! [*Disappears.*]

Person 6:   I wish I was in Alaska where it was freezing cold! [*Disappears.*]

Person 7:   I wish I was in Hawaii doing the hula with a cool chick. [*Disappears.*]

Person 8:   I wish I was home shooting some hoops with the guys! [*Disappears.*]

Person 9:   I wish I were home jammin' to my music, man! [*Disappears.*]

Person 10:   [*Looks around empty island.*] Wow. It's lonely. I wish all my friends were back here so I'd have someone to talk to.

The sound effect and light flickering start up again. This continues while all of the others spin back on the scene, each holding or wearing something indicating they were doing what they had wished. For example, the "shopper" would come on with multiple shopping bags, the "jammer" would come on with boom box and headphones, etc.

After everyone is back on stage, they look around in a confused manner, and then realize that Person #10 is the only one who conjured them back. They all glare at him, then chase him off the stage!

The End

Note: Other suggestions for wishes include the following:

- getting a manicure
- at the ballgame
- eating a steak dinner
- having a huge ice cream sundae
- taking a nice hot shower
- taking a ride in my new sports car.

The Amazing Caterpillar

This script is geared for younger groups. Characters: Caterpillar Trainer and Caterpillar.

The Caterpillar comprises 8 to 10 actors under blankets or sheets. Each actor should hold a noisemaker of some kind in one hand, leaving the second hand ready to pass items along under the blanket.

Trainer: [*These lines should be recited as if a ringmaster in a circus.*] You will now witness the most amazing feat ever seen in this country. This amazing caterpillar will eat anything I put in front of him. Now, we ask that members of the audience remain very quiet because we do not want to distract the caterpillar!

The Trainer then "feeds" the Caterpillar a box of cereal. The box, actually empty, is passed under the blanket from actor to actor, each actor making crunching, rattling noises. The audience will see movement as the Caterpillar "digests" the cereal. When it reaches the end of the line the empty box is thrown out of the back of the Caterpillar. The Trainer can give the Caterpillar other objects (whole apple goes in and just an apple core comes out, etc.). The Caterpillar is still hungry, so it swallows the Trainer! The Trainer is passed along (under or in back of) the blanket, and at the end all that comes out is a pair of pants and shirt that match what the Trainer was wearing. The Caterpillar belches and walks offstage.

It can be very funny if each actor emits a different "digestive sound" as the food is passed from front to back.

Suggestions for Caterpillar sound effects:

- Shake a box containing pebbles.
- Crumple noisy plastic wrap (empty potato chip bag).
- Ring a bell.
- Shake a maraca.
- Strike a wood block.
- Groan.
- Make a "raspberry" sound.
- Smack lips loudly.

The Zookeeper

This script is geared for younger groups. Characters: Zookeeper and any number of zoo animals. These can be simply suggested by hats with ears, etc.

Zookeeper: Ladies and Gentlemen, I would like you to meet our fabulous animals. First is the somersaulting tiger. [*Tiger does a somersault.*]

The zookeeper goes on to introduce each animal, talking about some feat that the animal can perform. These could include the following:

- *hopping on one foot*
- *picking something up with toe or nose*
- *touching elbow to ear*
- *rolling like a log*
- *walking backwards*
- *spelling*
- *counting to ten.*

The zookeeper then starts telling stories about the animals (see below for an example), and each time he mentions an animal, that animal performs their "trick." (For younger actors this should be short and scripted.) The animals look happy to perform at first, but soon grow tired of it, eventually chasing the zookeeper offstage!

Zookeeper: [*Running off.*] And then the animals turned on their zookeeper and he was never seen agaaaiinnnnn…

Sample story for "The Zookeeper"

The other day the most amazing thing happened here at the zoo. Just as the tiger somersaulted and the rhino did a ballet spin, there was a huge group of visitors who wanted to hear about the zoo. Every time I started to speak, the monkeys hopped on one foot and the parrot rolled like a log right in front of me. I would have tripped if it weren't for the zebra who was picking up food with its nose. I backed into the zebra just as the tiger and the rhino, the monkey, and the parrot did their tricks. Next thing you know, the zebra started up again and the monkey got in his way. The zebra thought it was funny and the tiger didn't think it was funny. I thought the tiger and the zebra and the monkey and the parrot and the rhino would finally be tired, but the tiger and the monkey and the zebra and the parrot and the rhino just kept doing their tricks until… [*Animals all stop, look at one another, then stare at zookeeper, then start chasing him.*] all the animals chased the Zookeeper and he was never seen agaaainnnn… [*Voice fading as he runs off stage with all of the animals following him.*]

Note: there are several ways to do the story.

1. It could be written out and read by one of your actors who is a fluent reader.

2. An adult or NT actor could read it.

3. An adult or NT actor could adlib it—this is the funniest way, because then even the actors aren't sure when their animal name will be mentioned, cueing them to perform.

Joke scripts

Doctor and Patient

Doctor: How are you getting along with those strength pills I gave you last week?

Patient: I don't know. I'm not strong enough to get the lid off the bottle yet.

No Test Today!

Joe: Hurrah! The teacher said we'd have a test today, rain or shine.

Matt: Then why are you so happy?

Joe: It's snowing!

Aunt

Rob: Did you know that my uncle's wife builds houses?

Steve: Oh, so she's a carpenter aunt!

Raining Cats and Dogs

Mandy: What do you see on the ground when it's raining cats and dogs?

Kim: Poodles!

A Cat Substitute

Jane: I'm sorry I ran over your cat.

Sam: It's OK. I'll get another one.

Jane: No, it's not OK. I'd like to replace your cat.

Sam: All right. How good are you at catching mice?

Banana in the Ear

Carolyn   John, you have a banana in your ear!

John: What did you say?

Carolyn: I said YOU HAVE A BANANA IN YOUR EAR.

John: I'm sorry. I can't hear you…I have a banana in my ear.

Spelling Lesson

Teacher: Please spell *mouse*.

Mary: M-O-U-S.

Teacher: But what's on the end?

Mary: A tail.

Hungry Pup

Ross: My dog ate my book! What should I do?

John: Take the words out of his mouth.

Round-up

Tex: Wanna hear a story about a cattle round-up?

Joe: Nah, HERD one, HERD 'em all!

Plane Jane

Jane: Did you hear the joke about the airplane?

Marty: No I haven't.

Jane: Ah, never mind, it's over your head.

Dirty Laundry

Chris: Hey, I heard that pigs do their own laundry.

Josh: That's hogwash!

References

Attwood, T. (1998) *Asperger Syndrome: A Guide for Parents and Professionals.* London: Jessica Kingsley Publishers.

Baker, J. (2003) *Social Skills Training for Children and Adolescents with Asperger Syndrome and Social Communication Problems.* Shawnee Mission, KS: Autism Asperger Publishing Company.

Baron-Cohen, S. and Bolton, P. (1993) *Autism: The Facts.* New York: Oxford University Press.

Bolick, T. (2002) *Asperger Syndrome and Adolescence.* Arlington, TX: Future Horizons.

Faherty, C. (2000) *Asperger's: What Does It Mean To Me?* Arlington, TX: Future Horizons.

Gray, C. (1998) *The Advanced Social Story Workbook.* Jenison, MI: Jenison Public Schools.

Myles, B. and Adreon, D. (2001) *Asperger Syndrome and Adolescence: Practical Solutions for School Success.* Shawnee Mission, KS: Autism Asperger Publishing Company.

Myles, B., Trautman, M. and Schelvan, R. (2004) *The Hidden Curriculum: Practical Solutions for Understanding Unstated Rules in Social Situations.* Shawnee Mission, KS: Autism Asperger Publishing Company.

Winner, M. (2000) *Inside Out: What Makes a Person with Social Cognitive Deficits Tick?* San Jose, CA: Michelle G. Winner.

Winner, M. (2002) *Thinking about You Thinking About Me.* San Jose, CA: Michelle G. Winner.

Resources

Art and Office Supplies

The following websites are places from which you can buy art and/or office supplies for your workshops.

www.abcschoolsupply.com

www.staples.com

www.becker.com

Costumes and Miscellaneous Props

Oriental Trading is a great place to buy hats, costume pieces, craft kits, and treasure box rewards at a very reasonable price.

www.orientaltrading.com

Ebay is a great resource when you are looking for something very specific and/or unusual. I have found some fun props/costumes there for reasonable prices.

www.ebay.com

Buycostumes.com has lots of costumes in kids and adult sizes available here if you have some type of budget.

www.buycostumes.com

This is the website you can access to find a **Goodwill store** near you. I have purchased many, many costumes from the clearance room at our local Goodwill. These have included girls', ladies' dresses, suit jackets, gowns, and much more.

http://locator.goodwill.org

Improvisational Activities, Scenes, Skits

There are many books available containing theater games, skits and scenes for your actors. Here are a few I would recommend:

Impro, by Keith Johnstone (Routledge, 1987), is a wonderful resource for leaders looking to understand the tenets of improvisation. Some of the concepts in this book might be beyond what you are doing in our workshops, but it is a great resource book for directors/instructors.

101 Improv Games for Children and Adults, by Bob Bedore, illustrated by Ian Barkley (Hunter House Publishers, 2004), contains many games and activities that can get your actors starting to think creatively.

The Skit Book, by Margaret MacDonald (August House, 2006), contains 101 "camp skits". These are short skits most often performed in camp settings, and collected by the author from children. They are short and silly, and the actors love them. They often have punch lines that have to do with multiple meanings or misunderstood language, making them great teaching tools for our actors. They are easily revised for a variety of cast sizes.

Get in the Act, by Shirley Ullom (Meriwether Publishing, Ltd., 1994), contains many monologues, dialogues and skits. This is a great resource for adolescent groups, offering pieces that can accommodate one to five actors.

Play Publishing Companies

When your group progresses and you want to find one-act or full-length plays, you might want to explore the following publishing houses.

Pioneer Drama Service has a variety of short and longer plays geared specifically toward school age populations.
www.pioneerdrama.com

Baker's Plays offers a comparable assortment of plays and theater resource books. This publisher offers a specific section on children's plays.
www.bakersplays.com

Eldridge Plays also contains plays and on-acts for both elementary and secondary age actors.
www.histage.com

If you have a group that is musically inclined, **J.W. Pepper** has a selection of musicals that range from 15 minutes to full length. These shows span all age groups, and most have a CD of recorded music, making teaching and learning the songs easy.
www.jwpepper.com

Other

Poems by **Shel Silverstein** are wonderful pieces for your younger actors to dramatize and illustrate. *Where the Sidewalk Ends* and *A Light in the Attic* are compilations of his whimsical and wonderful poems, and have been the source of many dramatizations in my younger groups. Having actors view his children's animated website is a great way to introduce his work.

www.shelsilverstein.com

Subject Index

Author Index